Praise for Danny Pellegrino

"Danny Pellegrino is as brilliant, sharp, and funny as they come. Enjoy his book and laugh your you-know-what off again and again."

—Drew Barrymore, *New York Times* bestselling author of *Wildflower*

"*The Jolliest Bunch* is a hilarious holiday horror show filled with heart. His essays make me feel seen, and I'm not just saying that because he mentions me on page 30. A must-read for anyone who lives for and loathes the holidays. Stuff your stockings with this book!"

—Kelly Ripa, *New York Times* bestselling author of *Live Wire*

"[Readers] will find themselves nodding along to Pellegrino's charming storytelling style and cringing on his behalf."

—*Booklist*

"Danny Pellegrino is a delight, and so are his stories!"

—*New York Times* bestselling author Andy Cohen

"Emotionally rewarding and wildly entertaining."

—*New York Times* bestselling author Megan McCafferty

"You will see some version of yourself in his words, journey, and truth. Not only will you laugh—and possibly cry—but you will also end up learning more about Danny and, inevitably, yourself."

—Rachel Lindsay, media personality and author of *Miss Me with That*

"Danny Pellegrino is a national treasure... His knowledge of pop culture is unrivaled and his humor is unmatched. I'm both happy for him and seething with jealousy."

—Casey Wilson, *New York Times* bestselling author of *The Wreckage of My Presence*

"Danny Pellegrino's exuberantly funny and poignant stories of growing up gay are stuffed with loving pop-culture references and laced with real emotion."

—*Shelf Awareness*

"I haven't laughed this hard reading a book *ever*. I'm talking full belly laughs and tears of joy. From a cross-country road trip gone off the rails to a paranormal experience in Hawaii, Danny Pellegrino's stories are absolutely priceless. They're poignant, too. *The Jolliest Bunch* evokes all the best holiday songs—the twinkle -lit joy and bittersweet nostalgia for Christmases past—and feels like catching up with an old friend over mugs of mulled wine or peppermint mochas. This book is hilarious and heartwarming all at once. I loved it and didn't want it to end!"

—Erin Carlson, author of *I'll Have What She's Having* and *Queen Meryl*

THE *Jolliest* BUNCH

Also by Danny Pellegrino

How Do I Un-Remember This?: Unfortunately True Stories

DANNY PELLEGRINO

This book is a memoir. It reflects the author's present recollections of experiences over a period of time. Some names and characteristics have been changed, some events have been compressed, and some dialogue has been re-created.

Published by Sourcebooks
P.O. Box 4410, Naperville, Illinois 60567-4410
(630) 961-3900
sourcebooks.com

Cataloging-in-Publication Data is on file with the Library of Congress.

Printed and bound in Canada.
MBP 10 9 8 7 6 5 4 3 2 1

"We're all in this together! This is a full-blown, four-alarm, holiday emergency here! We're gonna press on, and we're gonna have the hap-hap-happiest Christmas since Bing Crosby tap-danced with Danny fucking Kaye. And when Santa squeezes his fat white ass down that chimney tonight, he's gonna find *the jolliest bunch* of assholes this side of the nuthouse."

—CLARK GRISWOLD, *NATIONAL LAMPOON'S CHRISTMAS VACATION*

Contents

Introduction

I used to cry when Christmas ended. It was too sad for me, the thought of the holiday I looked forward to all year already being in the past, even though I was still in the throes of it. When the big day would wind down, I'd take my new toys to the bedroom and sob. Dad would be putting away the camcorder; Mom, cleaning the torn gift wrap; and my brothers, out in the snow. The tree would still be lit, and leftover food would be lukewarm on the counter, yet my insides would already be in turmoil. Where would all the excitement and joy go when the artificial tree was stuffed back in the basement? I was an emotional kid, who turned into an even more emotional adult—one who mourns the good times as much as he mourns the bad. Perfect days end with me wiping up the same tears that result from the crappy days. I feel lucky that *most* of my December 25ths found me in bed eulogizing a wonderful season and not upset that nothing in my life was as festive as Rankin/Bass.

The holiday season sucks for a lot of people, I get that. I'm not here to change your mind. I know plenty of people who avoid the red and green lights like a plague, treating them more like black-and-blue bruises, pain they must endure until they're healed in January. This book is for those people just as much as it is for the people who start singing "All I Want for Christmas Is You" in August. Many of you may not celebrate the customs and traditions set forth throughout these pages because of your religion or otherwise, but I hope you'll still find moments you recognize, like chaotic family gatherings or Halloweens gone wild. Let this be my Xmas (in the nonreligious sense) card to all of you. If you've had a handful of horror holidays, consider my tales trauma bonding. If you're a mean one (Mr. Grinch), so be it. Let these fables be a balm, an escape from the solitude of your wintry fortress. Let me be your Cindy Lou Who. The Santa to your elf. The ghost of Christmas past. Your unlikely angel! Turn on the leg lamp, and let me lasso you the moon.

Lips often curl upward when people cry, the same direction they go when you're smiling. There's a brilliant scene in the movie *Jerry Maguire* when Tom Cruise's character, Jerry, proposes to Renée Zellweger's Dorothy. She's wearing sunglasses, so you can't see her eyes. He asks her if she'll marry him, and her lips curl up, but Jerry (and the audience) doesn't know if she's happy or sad. When he removes her sunglasses, we're relieved to see in her eyes that she's thrilled. My point is sad times sometimes look like happy ones and vice versa. Christmas is like that. We look back fondly on tough times and romanticize the worst moments.

Sometimes it rains in December and snows on Halloween, but Hallmark wouldn't dare show us that. Either way, we muddle through and hope we find some laughs along the way. If you're someone who rejoices with the season, then rejoice with me as I tell you about my favorite tales from October to January. Light the fire, pour yourself some hot cocoa or eggnog, turn on the jazzy jingle bell music station, and read along under a cozy blanket. Don't be like me and cry because it's over; cry tears of laughter while it's happening. Don your gay apparel, and join me for the jolliest bunch of unhinged, unfortunately true-ish* stories.

---

* Names, locations, and other details have been altered to protect me from the wrath of loved ones.

The Night Before

'Twas the night before Christmas, and all through the house, not a creature was stirring, not even...

Wait—there was a creature stirring. Mom. And this story begins with her literally at the stove, stirring pasta sauce on Christmas Eve. Elsewhere in this book, I tell the tale of another mom who absolutely lost it over the course of Thanksgiving Day. You may be saying to yourself, "Danny, you can't possibly have multiple stories about a mom having a seasonal breakdown." Oh, but I do. I could probably fill a whole book exclusively with stories about moms going nuts because moms do it *all*. They decorate, they cook, and they make it nice! For all that work, they *deserve* to go a little berserk. THEY'VE EARNED IT. Not all families are made up of one mom and one dad, but there's usually one person in the family with hot mess holiday energy, so let's not focus on the gender of it all.

Okay, so back to Linda Pellegrino. She's going to kill me for telling this story, but of all the stories, this is the most important

Linda story that Linda ever Linda'd! Like the poster for JLo's 2002 thriller *Enough* says, "Everyone has a limit," and hers happened to be on Christmas Eve... Every. Single. Year. That's right, she loses it almost down to the exact minute (approximately 5:10 p.m. EST), right before the stockings are hung by the chimney with care and Santa squeezes his ass down to fill 'em. The meltdown begins at 5:10 p.m. EST because that's shortly after we hit the one-hour mark until her guests are due to arrive. Every year, she invites her side of the family over for cocktails, food, and music—which is usually of the "Jingle Bells" variety, but one year she accidentally put a 50 Cent CD in the disc player and didn't know how to change it. I was the only one who knew how to work the machine, and I was getting far too much enjoyment out of "In Da Club" playing while Mom plated her cookies, so the party listened to it in its entirety before I switched it to Michael Bublé.

When guests start arriving at the house around 6:00 p.m. EST, my mom already has her wine poured and is acting as though everything is picture perfect. She's full of energy and jolliness like one of the smiling hosts on the Food Network, serving Ina Garten moon and Giada De Laurentiis rising in her Christmas Eve astrological chart. The moments before that 5:10 to 5:59 p.m. EST window are when only a select few get to see the demon that lives inside her. It comes out exactly one time per year, and it's for approximately forty-nine minutes. It's kind of like *Gremlins*, only instead of becoming a monster from eating after midnight, Mom turns into a savage while she finishes making her world-famous potato salad and a bread-bowl spinach dip that is to die for (among many other things).

I still don't understand why she keeps throwing this party every year, because it seems like a nightmare for her. The stress of having her family over sends her up a wall, and she tries so hard for it to be perfect, even though the group would be happy with some pizza alongside free booze and a place to smoke. All she needs to do is set up a highball station so Grandma and company can get boozed up and reminisce.

"Be a good little boy and go make Grandma her highball," Grandma Sophie would say to me every year, not caring if I was six or sixteen, so long as she didn't have to bartend herself.

The company doesn't even need a garnish or anything fancy, just plastic cups with a gallon of ginger ale and cheap whiskey. That's it. But Mom insists on having a giant spread, making everything by hand, and driving me, my brothers, and Dad crazy before the guests arrive.

Doesn't matter how prepared we are for the Christmas Eve shindig, that morning is when the chaos starts and tensions rise, albeit to manageable levels.

Here's a rough timeline of the day:

6:11 a.m.: "Is everyone gonna sleep all day?! I need help! Yous all get to relax while I take care of the entire holiday! WAKE UP AND HELP ME," Mom says before the sun rises.

11:15 a.m.: My dad, brothers, and I are sent to the

store for a variety of items—booze, napkins, some obscure potato chip Mom insists Cousin What's-His-Name needs to have with the dip. Then we head to the funeral home for seating. (Everyone else rents chairs from the local funeral home, right?) I always assumed this was normal, but as I got older, I realized the morbidity of it all and questioned why my parents didn't invest in their own cheap chairs instead of getting the uncomfortable wooden fold-ups that people sit on while they're paying their respects to a loved one's rotting corpse. Those funeral chairs are loaded with sad memories and tears and dried gum, but we're always calling up Father Hendelkin to see if we can borrow them for a large family event. Dad drives us boys up to the funeral home and parks the car while we tiptoe past a service and ask where the chairs are. I guess they're free, but still, is it worth it? They aren't even padded. And we always have to return them the next day, so Dad is forced to drive us, hungover, on Christmas day to ensure the holiday crowd at the mortuary has ample seating for their send-offs.

1:45 p.m.: Once the free death chairs are picked up, we head back home, where Mom is manning multiple burners plus the oven and a separate roaster that plugs into a wall outlet. Her forehead glistens not because her inner aura is shining outward but because she's sweating like a whore in church. Even though it's snowing outside, a cold Ohio winter, the kitchen feels like the pits of hell because she's cooking so many things on various sources of heat. Ham, lasagna, cookies, pigs in a blanket, multiple dips that need to be heated. There are countless dips, but somehow none of the ones she serves are cold. On Easter, she makes a no-bake French onion dip that doesn't need any heat, but on Christmas Eve, she insists on exclusively hot dips. She cooks enough of these dips to feed a three-hundred-person wedding, but there are only about fifteen people outside my immediate family who show up. Mom has no sous-chef or assistance with the food because no one can cook to her standards; plus, she likes everyone knowing she makes it all herself. Occasionally, I'm asked to cut a block of Swiss cheese for a charcuterie tray, but she's never thrilled with the performance.

2:15 p.m.: "Why are you cutting it like that, Dan? Good thing I bought extra because I'm gonna have to redo it myself!" she says about the cubes of Swiss I cut as she wipes sweat off her brow.

The one food she does outsource is a sheet pizza, which stays in the laundry room. Was anyone else out there raised with a laundry room that doubles as a buffet table *and* a bar? Mind you, the laundry room isn't near the kitchen, so guests of the Pellegrinos have to haul ass across the main floor to get a piece of pizza and their Seven and Seven off the dryer.

Those guests not only make use of the laundry room,

but they also get to spend time in the cold-ass garage, which turns into a smoking lounge because Mom's side of the family is full of Marlboro lovers, and she doesn't let them smoke in the house. She places one space heater, two ashtrays, and approximately three funeral chairs in the closed garage for the family to smoke.

A lot of the rooms are repurposed for parties. Looking for a coat closet? Never heard of it. At our house, guests' outerwear goes into a child's bedroom, on top of the bed, piled vertically. It's a tradition that at least two people take the wrong jacket upon leaving. Cousin Irene once wore long johns under her pants, which she insisted she take off and leave on the twin bed with her jacket. At the end of the night, Aunt Helen accidentally took the wrong coat, but it was okay because she hadn't hung a stocking, and now she had Cousin Irene's long underwear to greet St. Nick.

4:00 p.m.: Before guests arrive, at least one of the Pellegrino boys sneaks into the laundry room, grabs one small square of the sheet pizza, scurries off into the cold garage, and eats it, thinking no one will catch on. Mom goes into the laundry room to fill the ice bucket, opens the pizza box, and notices the small square missing. It wouldn't matter if the sheet pizza were the size of a football field—she does NOT like it when we do that. This usually happens around 4:00, and it's like we all get a sneak preview of the devil that will appear later. If Ma's demon movie starts at 5:10, the 4:00 pizza debacle is the trailer.

While every single year is a nightmare, one particular Christmas Eve was a low point for Queen Linda, and to be honest, it's not entirely her fault. Dad added to the stress by disappearing midmorning, telling us all he had a surprise in store, while I took the other family car to run the yearly errands.

"I don't need a surprise, Gar! I need you to help me set up for the party!" Mom scolded.

"Trust me, you'll love it!" he replied.

Mom did not, in fact, love the surprise. Our dog had passed earlier that year, and my dad thought it would be a good idea to get a puppy, only Mom had no clue. Part of me thinks Dad just wanted to get out of picking up the chairs at the funeral home, so when he left for an "errand" and returned with an eight-week-old puppy, Mom was PISSED (and I was tired from having to carry extra seating from the undertaker's establishment).

I *love* dogs, but puppies are a lot of work, and this one added yappy chaos to a chaotic household. (And maybe don't get an eight-week-old puppy on the one day a year Mom has her routine nervous breakdown?) Before Mom could even scold her husband, the pup pooped and crawled under the Christmas tree. Dad went to grab him, and the whole tree toppled over.

"Timber!" Dad playfully yelled.

You know when parents get so mad that they're almost calm? Like, they're past the point of mad and have a chilling stillness to them? Mom had that. She let out the quietest "Gary, return the dog." Every syllable was pronounced, but you could barely hear her over the sounds of the barks and stove work happening inside the kitchen. It was like Meryl Streep as Miranda Priestly in *The Devil Wears Prada*; she's scarier *because* she's quiet. Dad and the dog got out of there immediately, which left Mom with even more items on her to-do list while Dad was driving hours across the state to where he got the adorable pooch.*

Dad recruited my brother Bryan to go with him, Junior drove off to pick up his girlfriend, and I retreated into the basement for some quiet time before the cousins arrived.

Just as my eyes began to close for a nice midday slumber amid my seventy-fifth viewing of *Home Alone* (that year), I heard something upstairs. There arose such a clatter, and my senses alerted to see what was the matter. I looked at the clock and noticed it was 4:55 p.m., so I assumed I had at least fifteen more minutes to power nap before the demon arrived.

"AHHhhh!" I heard Mom scream. I worried perhaps she was hurt or maybe dropped something. I ran upstairs.

"Ma? Ma, where are you?" I asked.

No one was there. The stove was on, but she wasn't in the kitchen. The Carpenters Christmas album was playing in the living room, but there was no sign of the matriarch of the family. I knocked on her bedroom door, but there wasn't a creature

* I know it's not right to adopt a dog and then unadopt it. I'm certainly not proud of the Pellegrino family for doing so, but THIS IS (unfortunately) OUR TRUTH. Dad isn't on social media, but you can direct your anger to him via carrier pigeon or telegram if you feel so inclined.

stirring in there either. Finally, I heard something coming from the garage—a car starting. I knew it was too soon for Dad to be back. I thought maybe Mom was moving her vehicle so she could set up the smoking section, but she was just sitting in the driver's seat. I put on the nearest pair of shoes, my dad's two-sizes-too-small snow boots, and hobbled over to the car window.

"Ma, what are you doing?"

"I'm goin' to the corner, Dan!" she said through tears.

"Open the car! Let me in!"

"No, I'm goin' to the corner!"

"Did you forget something at the store? Do you want me to run out?" I asked.

"No, I'm not goin' to the corner store. I'm goin' to the corner. Just goin'."

"What do you mean, Ma?"

"I'm goin', Dan! I'm leaving the house!" she shouted through the window.

"What about the food? You left the oven on—"

"Yous can do all the food, and yous can do the whole Christmas without me because I'm goin' to the corner. I've had it, Dan!"

This was when I finally realized she wasn't running an errand—she was having the breakdown early and worse than the other years. *The corner* was the manifestation of that breakdown. I'm not sure she had an exact corner in mind or that she ever planned to leave the driveway; Mom just wanted people to notice how much stress she was under. We had all gone through the motions for so many years, sneaking the pizza she so badly wanted to present as whole, running off to get dogs she didn't want, and retreating to the basement for naps when she was at her busiest. She didn't want to *ask* us to help; she just wanted us to do it.

"I'm sorry I didn't come upstairs. What do you need me to do?" I asked.

"You don't have to do anything. Christmas is canceled. I'll be at the corner, Dan!" she replied.

Mom needed to be seen, to be acknowledged, and to be appreciated, like all mothers do. Rather than ask specifics about what corner she was referring to or what she would do once she was there, I shut my mouth and got her to unlock the car. I sat in the passenger seat next to her, and the car remained in neutral as Mom caught her breath and the Rudolph-red coloring drained from her face. We sat in silence for about two minutes, and then she took one deep breath and went back inside. While she reapplied her makeup, I took over food-stirring duties, mixing the sauce and basting the ham. Dad finally arrived back home, and I filled him in. Mom eventually returned to the kitchen looking more stunning than ever and didn't say hi to her husband or explain the outburst. She simply turned up the Christmas music to drown out the devil that was exiting her body, right on schedule. As her final tear dried, the doorbell rang.

"Hon, do you mind getting the door? Must be my sister Joanne," she said calmly to Dad as if nothing had happened.

Dad and I looked at each other, wondering if the demon

was completely exorcised for the season or simply waiting to strike again. Dad opened the front door and welcomed his sister-in-law.

"Merry Christmas!" Aunt Joanne said.

"Joannie, Merry Christmas!" Mom called to her oldest sibling.

As Aunt Joanne made her way to the kitchen and saw the extensive spread of food and Christmas decor, she hugged my mom. "Everything looks great! You did too much, Lin."

"It was nothing. You know I love the holidays," Mom said with a smile.

More guests streamed in and complimented the party Linda Pellegrino had put together, commenting on how beautiful everything looked, how flawless all the homemade goodies tasted, and how one human had made a gathering so festive. They had all grown up with her, so they knew she was the one who threw it all together, and although we picked up a bottle of booze here and there and rented some dead people's seating, it was Mom's party. Every time someone let out an "mmmm" after a bite of food or an "oooohhh" after seeing a dancing Santa or twinkle light in the living room, Mom would respond with a simple, "It was nothing," alongside that beautiful smile.

It was something. Now that I'm older and have thrown my own holiday functions, I get it. We are all Linda this time of year. So to all the moms and mom-adjacent people, those who are throwing parties they don't really want to have, making sure everyone is well fed and has a place to smoke their cigs, take a moment to pop your emotional cork like Linda does around

5:10 p.m. EST, but just for a moment. Some years, you might need to cleanse that spirit a few minutes earlier, and that's okay. Otherwise, it simmers inside you like the pot of sauce on your burner, threatening to boil over and make a mess that you don't have time to clean up. Scream inside the parked car in your garage or even into a nearby pillow. Drive away to the corner, yell at your kids, call your husband an asshole, and then get back to party planning so that when your guests arrive, they can see how festive you made it. And when they say, "I don't know how you do it all," you can respond with, "It was nothing," even though everyone knows you're lying.

Saint Claudia of Reseda

"I gots some stray capigool and prosciut in my purse if ya hungry."

These words floated out of my new friend's mouth about seventeen minutes into our cross-country road trip. Her name was Claudia, and she was an Italian American woman in her late forties from Reseda, California, and she was driving me from the West Coast back to Ohio for Christmas. She was equal parts all her idols: Madonna, Marisa Tomei's character in *My Cousin Vinny*, and Sophia from *The Golden Girls*. We were basically strangers, tied only by the fact that she worked at an optometrist's office with my buddy Heather. Heather knew I wanted to get back to the Midwest on a budget and heard that Claudia was driving cross-country to visit her ex-boyfriend (Evan) near my hometown, so I strapped in for an adventure with a woman I'd just met who carried deli meat in her purse and drove a 2001 Montero Sport.

"I packed a Kind bar and some fruit snacks, so I'm okay for a little while, thanks," I replied.

"The meats should stay good through Colorado. I brought an ice pack for 'em. And I know a bunch of restaurants on the way we can stop at if you get hungrier."

The drive across the country is brutal, and I'm not sure what I was thinking spending days in a car with a woman I didn't know, convinced the couple of hundred dollars I saved would be worth the multiple days I had with Claudia, whose purse-meat aroma was quickly spreading throughout the car with thirty-four hours left on our expedition. I could barely focus on the scent as my senses were preoccupied with listening to her sing along to the Christmas with the Rat Pack playlist she'd programmed. Maybe the vocals would've been bearable if her nasally voice weren't singing "joyful all yeast onions rise" instead of "joyful all ye nations rise" during "Hark! The Herald Angels Sing."

"Are you singing…'yeast onion'?" I asked her.

"Yeah, 'yeast onions.'"

"The lyric is 'all ye nations rise.'"

"No, yeast makes things rise, so they are singing about cookin'," Claudia corrected.

The meat and the singing were both red flags, but being the people pleaser I am, I decided to ignore these signs and instead try to make the best of it. I sang along to Frank Sinatra while eating my packaged fruit snacks. The upside was that Claudia had a zero-f's attitude, reminded me a bit of my grandma, and could probably help me let loose a little before I spent a week with my family.

"So you're going to see a guy in Ohio?" I asked.

"Yeah, an ex-boyfriend and a real charmer. He's a real estate agent, he drives an H2, and he's packin'," she bragged.

When she said he was "packin'," I assumed she was talking about his penis. Something that happens when you're an out gay man is that people talk to you about sex and men's bodies *a lot*. Women will open up about the men they date almost instantly upon meeting you. I've met gals at bars who are telling me about their husband's junk while waiting in line for the restrooms. Every interaction between a gay man and straight woman becomes a scene from *Sex and the City*, and the Charlottes become Samanthas as soon as they find out you're homosexual—and it's one of the best parts about being a gay man.

"Congrats, girl! Does this guy know what to do with what he's packin' though?" I asked.

I admit my response was a little cringe, what with the *girl* and suddenly asking about how good this man is in the sack, but life is short, and we had a long drive ahead.

"Yeah, he points it at my forehead when we hook up. It is so hot."

Okay, now I was a bit confused. Sure, I could picture the logistics of a man pointing his Jack Nicholson at a woman's face, but the way she said it made me think we were on two different pages.

"So, like, when you're going down on him, he stops to point it at your forehead?" My question was gross but necessary.

"Sometimes, but sometimes he gives it to me when I'm riding him on top. He loves it."

I was officially lost. I didn't necessarily want to know more, but I needed to understand the logistics of what Claudia was talking about.

"Wait, so when you said he was packin'..."

"A gun. My man takes out a gun when we have sex."

My body immediately tensed up. I could feel my shoulder blades tighten and my butthole clench. Sweat dripped from my brow, and my eyes went wide as she continued.

"We point the gun at each other. It's not loaded, but it's so hot. Ooh, I better turn on the air—"

I don't want to kink shame. At all. However, I hadn't met anyone who was into gunplay during sex, so it caught me a bit off guard. Couple that with the fact that I was just meeting this woman, and I was a teensy bit concerned.

DANNY: Heather, who is this person you set me up with? Do you know anything about Claudia?

As I waited for my buddy to respond to my text, Claudia changed the subject. She started telling me about the gifts she'd bought for Evan's kids, whom he shared with an ex. Claudia was bringing them two toys inspired by Disney's *Tangled* as holiday presents in hopes they would like her. I say *inspired by*, because when I saw them in the back seat, it was clear they were knockoffs. The doll Claudia bought for her ex-boyfriend's daughters looked more like Michael Moore than Mandy Moore. There was dirt on the princess's face that resembled stubble, and instead of a cute chameleon sidekick like the character has in the movie, there was a generic plastic frog with a voice box that unleashed barks instead of ribbits.

"Aren't they cute?" Claudia asked.

"Yeah, but these aren't actually from the movie. They look like other characters," I said.

"SHIT!" she yelled at the top of her lungs.

I thought Claudia was yelling because of something on the road or because she forgot something back home, like turning off the curling iron or closing her garage.

"Shit, you think my gifts are trash? Fuck! Shit, shit, shit!" Her voice kept getting louder and more antagonistic. Just as my confusion was turning into fear, I got a ding on my phone. It was a text from Heather...

HEATHER: lol she's new at work, the only thing I know

> about her is she was driving to Ohio and she's on medication to quit smoking. Same one my ex took to quit. Made him nuts! Mood swings like crazy. How's it going?

At least I had an explanation for Claudia's shifting behavior, but we were still just on hour one of our drive! How was I to survive thirty-something more hours with this deranged human with a meat locker and affinity for gunplay?

"Omigod, no, Claudia! These gifts are *so* cute. Seriously way cuter than the regular *Tangled* toys. These are, like…unique," I lied.

"Okay, good, because I wanna impress this guy's kids. I haven't met the daughters yet."

Claudia then reached into her purse, felt her way through the pastrami, and pulled out a pack of Marlboros.

"Mind if I smoke? I'm trying to quit."

I don't like the smell of smoke, but I'd endure anything to keep the rage at bay.

"Go ahead! So how long have you been seeing this Evan guy?"

"Off and on for twenty-five years," she said as she took a drag.

"Five years?"

"No, twenty-five years. I met him in high school on a family vacation to Hilton Head."

I'm no relationship expert, but it seems to me that if someone hasn't been a good fit in twenty-five years, it may be time to move on, let the relationship go, but instead, Claudia packed up some deranged dolls and drove twenty-three hundred miles to see him. Different strokes for different folks, I suppose!

"He must be excited to see you," I said.

"He don't know I'm coming."

"So you're surprising him and his two daughters..."

"Five. He has five of 'em total. And a son."

"Oh, I didn't realize. I just saw the two toys back there—"

"Oh, I only got gifts for the two girls. Six would've been too pricey, and I thought one would've made me look cheap."

"You're surprising him and his...*six*...kids on Christmas?"

"Yeah, he's gonna flip!"

I admired the audacity, even if the gift logic was questionable. As a Libra, I rarely take leaps of faith or go out of my comfort zone, so I can only imagine how nervous I would be to show up (uninvited) somewhere and spurn two-thirds of the children I wanted to make a good impression on. But Claudia was wired different.

"I just hope he got me something because it's my birthday today."

"Your birthday is today? Omigod, Claudia, I feel bad you're driving when you should be celebrating."

"Don't feel bad. I got drunk earlier."

"Oh, you went out last night?"

"No, this morning I had some cocktails. Forty-seven, here I come!"

Whoopi Goldberg once said, "Molly, you in danger, girl," a quote that reverberated in my head as soon as I learned that Claudia was maybe drunk driving me across the country. I spent a moment trying to figure out what her blood-alcohol level might be by this point in the drive—and I optimistically assumed it was at least a little below the legal limit—a thought that quickly got derailed when I started thinking about it being her birthday. December 19. Of course she's a Sagittarius! And she was the most Sagittarius of Sagittariuses I'd ever met. Spontaneous, adventurous, a traveler. This explained Claudia to a tee. I'm not quite sure what the charts say about the driving drunk part (which we DO NOT condone and is inexcusable), but I said a silent prayer and offered the only two words I could think of...

"Happy birthday!"

The kind regards left my lips, and I began plotting my way off the highway of hell. Perhaps I'd fake an emergency and ask to be dropped off at the nearest airport, or maybe I'd just ghost her. She would get in her car at a rest stop after picking up some grub, and I would be gone. She'd assume I was the ghost of Christmas past, and she would prep herself for the present and future to join her as she drove the rest of the way while fighting a nicotine addiction.

By the time we reached Arizona, Claudia had sobered up, and it was time to stop for gas. We pulled up to the pump, and I went inside while Claudia filled the tank. My great escape would have to wait as this location was a little too sketch for ghosting purposes. It was in the middle of nowhere, and I couldn't risk being stranded at a gas station located on the side of a highway or trust that an Uber would find me. Somehow, I concluded Claudia would be safer, so I looked for snacks to last me until our next stop. I picked up some Doritos and a Diet Coke, then walked over to the red-cream holiday Oreos when suddenly—

"Don't move," Claudia whispered, lips literally grazing the back of my ear. She'd snuck up behind me like the quietest chaos agent. I didn't even hear her come in, and I certainly wasn't ready for what came next.

"I thought you pay at the pump. Why are you in here—"

"Shh! Don't say anything," she commanded.

I caught my reflection in the small mirror attached to the sunglasses stand and noticed both the fear in my eyes and that some of her maroon lipstick had rubbed off on my lobe.

"I'm gonna stick some stuff in your pocket. Act natural," she said.

"Claudia—"

She stuffed something into the back of my jeans, something big and round.

"Please, I—"

"QUIET, DANNY!" she shouted loud enough that the clerk could hear, but the gentleman behind the counter only briefly looked up from reading his ESPN magazine before deciding to ignore the hoopla.

Claudia's words left me shell-shocked. I was somehow mid-theft, against my will, but I was afraid that if I resisted, she would make things worse.

"Go to the car, and I'll pay for the gas. Go!" she instructed.

"But I can pay for my stuff. I just want a Diet Coke—"

"Go!"

I listened to her marching orders, but I set down my chips and pop, then scurried back to the getaway car. I figured I should only steal what she was forcing me to steal and not the items I had planned to purchase.

The next couple of minutes felt like a lifetime as I waited in the passenger seat for Claudia to join me, wondering if some local authorities would book her and then come for me. I was so nervous she wouldn't make it out of there, I almost forgot she had slipped the goods into my back pocket.

I reached back, nervous about what I'd find. Had she stolen another patron's wallet, or maybe she had taken something from inside the store when I wasn't looking? It felt like something round and papery, and it was. It was literally balled-up paper towels from the dispenser near the windshield washer.

Claudia finally arrived back in the driver's seat and turned on the car. "Ready to get back on the road?" she asked with a smile.

"Claudia, what did you put in my pocket? Did you wrap something up? Because all that's here is paper towel. Did something fall out? What if—"

"Yeah, I was just freakin' you out. I put some garbage I found in your pocket. You shoulda saw your face!"

"So I didn't steal anything?"

"No, but I stole a Snickers. You want half?"

"No, I wanted the Doritos, Diet Coke, and Oreos that I was going to pay for!"

"I have meats in my bag if you want."

"So you get to eat your stolen Snickers, but I'm supposed to just eat your purse meats?"

"Snickers is a sweet. You were buying savory, and that's a waste of money when I got perfectly good meats."

Some people are impossible to figure out. They zig when you think they're gonna zag. Claudia was like that, and I couldn't take it any longer. But unfortunately, every time I would think of a way out, she would bamboozle me into staying with her. We stopped in Kansas to spend the night, and I was convinced that was when I would leave her and catch a flight, but she somehow convinced me to put my belongings in a safe at the motel we stopped at and then dragged me to a local dive bar for Long Island iced teas. The next morning, I was so hungover that I didn't have the energy to find a way out. I was even desperate enough to eat some of her aged meats as we made our way through Missouri.

Somewhere along the way, before I could devise a proper exit strategy, I began to sorta like Claudia. Sure, she was a hot mess, her car smelled like antipasti mixed with White Diamonds, and her mood shifted quicker than I could keep up with, but she kept me on my toes! She was brass, bawdy, and honest, and I always keep my life very controlled. It was nice to be with someone different.

Everywhere we stopped, she would make both friends *and* enemies, but she was content with either. If I feel like someone doesn't like me, I stress to the point that I lose sleep over it, but Claudia just kept on driving to her destination without a care in the world. There was a bartender who gave us free drinks because she thought Claudia was a riot, a waitress who called Claudia the c-word after she stole the waitress's pen, and a police officer who let us go with a warning for doing eighty-five in a sixty because Claudia made him laugh. It was a roller coaster of interactions, and I was loving the ride.

By the time we reached Ohio, I was cramped and tired but enamored with Claudia's steadfast sense of self. She drove up to my parent's house, and I prepared my goodbye, a goodbye I'd planned on making much sooner but was glad I waited until we reached the finish line. In *A Christmas Carol*, Scrooge is visited by three ghosts who teach him a bunch of stuff about life, and Claudia was that for me. She drove me to my past, taught me to enjoy the present, and showed me what life could be in the future if I stopped caring so much about trying to be the person I think everyone wants me to be. Yes, she was a thief, a liar, and a person who enjoyed her sex with a side of firearms, but no one is perfect.

On December 24, I got a text.

CLAUDIA: Hey, going back to LA early. Turns out Evan's married. Oops! Lol. Let me know if you need a ride. Merry Christmas!

Of course Evan was married. And of course Claudia drove all the way across the country for him without knowing if he was single. I took a return flight back to California a week later, and the next time I texted Claudia, her number was out of service. Heather said Claudia stopped showing up for work, so I don't know where she is now, but every December, I think about my Sagittarius queen and hope she's doing what she loves...shoplifting, singing old-timey Christmas songs about yeast onions, and having (consensual) violent sex with a man she doesn't know well at all.

The Ghostly Duo

A gay man who died in the 1980s has been haunting me on Halloween my entire adult life. There, I said it! That's right, my name is Danny Pellegrino, and I have a homosexual ghost chasing me around on the spookiest holiday. Feels good to finally get that off my chest.

Being in touch with otherworldly spirits is quite a controversial topic. Brave celebrities like Vanessa Hudgens, Kesha, Demi Lovato, and Theresa Caputo have all been loud and proud about their connection to the deceased, but I've never quite been able to live my truth...until now. Every October 31, my queer celestial visitor rears his fabulous translucent head and spends the October holiday alongside me.

Ghostly guides are nothing new. Any fan of the 1995 feature film *Casper* knows that sometimes even ghosts have ghosts. In that movie, Casper is a friendly ghost, but he's spending his death being haunted by his own personal phantoms in the form of his uncles, known as the Ghostly Trio. These three grown-slash-dead men each have their own unique names, which I'm going to need approximately forty-five minutes to unpack: Stretch, Stinkie, and Fatso. According to the rules of the Casper lore, these are the characters' actual birth names, *not* nicknames. If we are to assume the friendly ghost was named Casper before he kicked the bucket and the other characters who straddle the line between living and dead also retain their earthly names when they become phantoms, then *logically* the uncles' birth certificates must name them as Stretch, Stinkie, and Fatso.

Ignoring for a moment that only a truly heinous parent would name their child *Fatso*, there are still so many mysteries to unpack with this paranormal family. If Casper's grandparents would name their children *Stretch*, *Stinkie*, and *Fatso*, then what were the names of Casper's father or mother? And how were Casper's parents able to escape ghostdom and proceed to a proper afterlife unlike the rest of the fam? I'm always blown away by siblings who somehow survive an unlikely fate.

Sometimes you meet someone who has it all together, only to learn they have a brother or sister who is a complete mess. Somewhere along the way, they veered from their bloodline. It's unclear if Stretch, Stinkie, and Fatso were Casper's uncles of the maternal or paternal variety, but either way, they were stuck in the in-between with a boy who died at such a young age and still managed to remain friendly.

I can only assume those slovenly and rude uncles are heterosexual, as they have no respect for Christina Ricci or a cameo from Amy Brenneman on the big screen. (Side note: if you haven't seen *Casper* in a while, go watch it immediately. It's crazy. I also believe it would've had a larger cultural footprint if the three uncles were three aunts played by iconic actresses like in *Hocus Pocus*, but that's a theory for another time.)

I didn't see a *gay* ghost on screen or off until I was a teenager. Casper does turn into Devon Sawa at the end of the movie, and though I wished Devon were gay and wanted to run off with me when I saw it as a young boy, that, alas, was not meant to be—which is why it was even more surprising when I discovered a gay ghost took a liking to me post puberty.

The first sign of my personal queer apparition was Halloween 2002ish. I was a teenager: too old to be trick-or-treating and not old enough to be out at a party. Instead, I was stuck in the in-between, passing out candy as the holiday episodes of *Roseanne* played on the TV. My parents were at their adult function, my older brothers were already off at college, and I was sneaking into the liquor cabinet for a "cocktail," drinking the first thing I found, which was some green liquor my cousin had illegally mailed from another country. I was home alone with obscene amounts of chocolate and booze, and a steady stream of kids dressed as vampires and Powerpuff Girls were knocking at the door for sweets.

In the suburbs of Ohio, trick-or-treating wraps up at an early hour. Occasionally, you get a straggler, but typically, you're done at 10:00 p.m. By 10:15, I was still wide awake and out of episodes to watch on Nick at Nite, so when the doorbell rang, I was ready to send them away and turn off the porch light so I could be left in peace with my green drink.

"Candy is done! Now scram," I said, sounding like an '80s movie villain.

When I opened the door and looked down, expecting to see a young person looking for a fun-size Snickers (we never gave out the full-size candy bars), I instead saw a VHS tape. I looked to my right and then to my left...no one was nearby. The streets were quiet. I picked up the tape, and it was a copy of *9 to 5*, the 1980 film starring Jane Fonda, Lily Tomlin, and Dolly Parton. Quite possibly the most gay-friendly cast ever assembled! While I was still in the closet at the time, I was no stranger to lady-led entertainment. It's imperative to remind you that *Stepmom* was in high rotation; I even used to bring a version I taped off the TV with us on family vacations, assuming my parents and two brothers would want to watch a drama about a dying mother while we were getting away from life's troubles on a Florida beach. Even so, I hadn't yet seen *9 to 5*. Rather than question how or why it had arrived at my feet, I simply went to the living room and put it into the VCR. I was enamored. Obsessed even. The thought crossed my mind that perhaps a spirit had delivered the goods, but I wasn't yet convinced.

Cut to a couple of years later, while in my sophomore year of college at Ohio University, when a group of us decided to take a trip to the Ridges to celebrate Halloween. The Ridges in Athens, Ohio, was formerly known as the Athens Lunatic Asylum, a hospital for people who suffered from various mental illnesses. Students would take trips to the abandoned Ridges at night because it was widely thought to be a haunted location. We gathered our flashlights and cocktail-filled water bottles, drove up once it was dark, and inspected the building, which was filled with old desks and supplies from years prior. Needless to say, it was spooky. During the visit, I shined a light on a rickety desk used for kids who had been schooled at the asylum. There was something scribbled on the chair. I called my friend Tina over to help me read it, but when she arrived with her own flashlight, the markings disappeared. She quickly turned her attention somewhere else, and when I looked back down, there it was! Scribbled on a seat...

If you can't say anything nice about anybody, come sit by me, it read. A *Steel Magnolias* quote! Right there, written in the empty loony bin—one of the most haunted places on earth! Of course, this was a film I *was* familiar with, a 1989 classic starring Sally Field, Julia Roberts, Shirley MacLaine, Olympia Dukakis, Daryl Hannah, and, once again, Dolly Parton. At this point, I was convinced there was a Dolly stan visiting me from the beyond.

Over the years, late October would hit, and I would keep an eye out for the signs of my gay ghost. There was a costume party in my midtwenties where I saw seven women and two men dressed as Jennifer Beals from *Flashdance,* and when I tried to gather them all for a picture, only *one* of the men could be found. He kept saying he was the only man dressed in that costume at this party, but I was certain I peed next to another drag Jennifer Beals because I remember he tried to pick me up in the bathroom, and I *never* forget someone who tries to pick me up in a restroom. Sexual advances next to a toilet are too personal to forget. Although this experience didn't provide any additional support for my Dolly Parton theory, it did prove I was being haunted.

The next encounter occurred in my early thirties. I took my niece and nephew trick-or-treating with my older brother, and as we were walking the suburban northeast Ohio street, I noticed something familiar. I was staying at my brother's house for the week, and his bar was filled with all sorts of unused bottles of booze, so I'd peeped a familiar green one, mixed it with Sprite, and poured it into a *Super Mario* to-go mug. As we were walking, I heard someone whispering, "Snap out of it!" in my ear over and over.

"Do you hear that?" I said to my eight-year-old niece.

"I don't hear anything," she said.

"You don't hear a man talking like Cher in *Moonstruck*?"

"What's *Moonstruck*?" she said, making the case for straights not being allowed to raise children.

Was I having a mental break? Possibly. Maybe. Probably. Likely. But I heard a Cher impression in my ear plain as day while holding a Mario mug full of liquor!

That's four different Halloweens! Four! Four times I was presented with ghostly information centered around 1980s chick flicks. I had my suspicions about a gay ghost, but of course, I couldn't be certain. That is, until the most recent Halloween.

What I'm about to tell you is heavy. If you're driving, pull over. You'll never be able to un-remember this. If you're someone who is spooked easily, I recommend skipping to the next chapter because I can't be responsible for the nightmares you will endure after I tell you this next tale.

It was a different kind of All Hallows' Eve, one spent on the island of Maui in Hawaii. My boyfriend Matt and I opted to get away from the hustle and bustle of our everyday lives and unwind on a sandy beach adjacent to a Four Seasons. I love going on vacation over holidays. There's something extra relaxing about it. It almost feels naughty, like you're doing something you're not supposed to.

When we got to Hawaii, the resort was quiet. There were a few families, with a small handful of kids at the pool wearing costume sunglasses that made them look like wolves and fairies, but mostly, there was nary a sign of Halloween in sight. Palm trees and macadamia nuts replaced the traditional broomsticks and Kit Kats. I spent the afternoon doing my favorite spooky season activity: watching every daytime talk show host wearing absurd costumes. I *live* to see *TODAY* show anchors in prosthetics that make them look like Charlie Brown characters or the fabulous Kelly Ripa in Harley Quinn cosplay while interviewing whatever celeb has a movie out that week.

As the sun set on October 31, my significant other and I retreated to a nearby luau, where we were seated with three other couples, including one who said they too were from the Midwest, a man and woman in their late sixties named Rod and Shelly, who looked broken and empty, like the shells of sunflower seeds found in the dugout of a baseball field. Almost immediately upon meeting me, Shelly mentioned the first time she and Rod made love freshman year of college after a football game. She also told me she and her roommates would smear lipstick on the door if one of them had a guy over and that by spring semester, it looked like "a doorway to a clown's dressing room" because Rod would spend so many nights with her. I hope those poor roommates are doing well now. Point is Shelly and Rod were both fun and wildly forthcoming, as the most interesting people always are.

"We snuck some hooch in here," Rod whispered under his stank breath as he pointed to his rusty flask. Shelly, meanwhile, was already overserved, inexplicably talking to the saltshaker as if it were one of her oldest and dearest friends.

I need you to know I would *never* drink from a stranger's cup; it's a terrible thing to do, and no one should ever do it, and I certainly would never drink from an unknown flask... unless I'm on vacation, in which case, I'll put my lips around just about anything (ladies, amiright?). What we hadn't realized when buying the tickets was that it was a *dry* luau, so the only alcohol was courtesy of this man named Rod, who told me every time there was a microphone within ten feet that he'd manually removed his tooth filling. I'm no lush, but I like a few cockies when I'm on holiday, so I let Rod fill my island pineapple juice with his own juice and made my way to the buffet.

In high school, they nicknamed me Two-Drink Danny because after a couple of cups, I was either dancing on a table or asleep. No middle ground. One of the benefits of not drinking a lot is that you can get drunk for cheap, but that also means you are in an unpredictable danger zone each time you indulge.

After just one of Rod's really strong punches, I was in dance-on-table mode. The event had a live band, so this is where I regretfully tell you all that I did ask them to play "I Put a Spell on You" in honor of the spooky holiday. They were kind enough to play the *Hocus Pocus* version, and I assume white people dancing to a seasonal Disney song in Maui is why *The White Lotus* struck a chord with so many viewers, because everyone got way too excited to hear Bette Midler singing on the loudspeaker. We shouldn't be allowed anywhere.

Eventually, I tuckered out. As I said my goodbyes to Rod and Shelly, he bamboozled me into taking one last shot of his magic potion. I obliged—and noticed it had a familiar taste when not mixed with pineapple juice—before I stumbled off to my room with my (sober) boyfriend, who, much like every night of a vacation, found himself exhausted by me.

"Yamikipiyabo, sub saray, I see do. See do!" I said to him, neither one of us knowing what it meant.

"You're too drunk," he said as I fell onto the bed. Before I knew it, he was snoring next to me, and my mind was racing. I had to get out of the room and explore the island; my buzz was calling me to do so.

I tiptoed out of the crisp hotel sheets and into the airport flip-flops I bought for too much money when I realized I left my own pair under my bed back home. Quietly, I made my way to the beach, where I found a group of young people carving pumpkins. Things are a bit fuzzy from here on out, so forgive me. The next order of events was roughly as follows:

Pumpkin carving.

A shot?

Sand.

I flipped my shorts inside out.

I drunk dialed my friend Beth.

I flipped my shirt inside out.

I swam (whether it was in the pool or ocean is unclear).

Before I knew it, it was the next morning. The sun rose on

November 1, and the waves crashing against the sand woke me right up. Rather than spooning with my loved one, I was cuddling a carved and soggy pumpkin ON THE BEACH. A carved and soggy pumpkin that simply read, *Fred*. My clothes were inside out, and my phone was dead. How did I get there? What happened? Why was the pumpkin all wet? I had no choice but to piece together what happened from the few clues I had. My boyfriend didn't even know I hadn't been in the room, so he wouldn't be much help. My phone battery was shot, so until it charged, I wouldn't have a tech trail to examine. I plugged it into the wall back in the room and headed to the hotel breakfast buffet. Maybe some food in me would help jog my memory, I figured.

While I was loading up on obscene amounts of mango and French toast, I noticed a table of twentysomething women giggling and looking my way.

"DP!" one of the young ladies yelled.

"Hi! Do I know you?"

"Omigod, you don't remember? We partied last night on the beach!" she said.

"Ugh, I'm sorry. I had some sketchy drink at dinner, and I don't remember much of anything from last night," I mentioned.

"You and Fred were wild!" she exclaimed with a loud cackle.

Shit, I thought. First Fred's name appeared on the pumpkin, and now a messy twentysomething was saying he and I were wild together! I was on this vacation with the love of my life—the last thing I wanted to do was cheat on him with some floozy vacation slut named Fred!

"Is Fred...here? What does he look like?" I asked, hoping that if I cheated on the man I was committed to spending the rest of my life with, maybe it was at least with someone who looked like Channing Tatum (fingers crossed)!

"Beats me," she said. "You kept telling us a man named Fred was with you, but you were all alone. You were singing something called 'Endless Love,' but you kept telling us you were only doing the Lionel Richie parts because Fred was there singing the Diana Ross parts. You were really fucked up."

Unfortunately, that story sounds like me, so I took her word for it. I've been known to force people to listen to me sing duet ballads when I'm drunk, only I normally have a singing partner in the flesh. The idea that I was just doing half a song for a full audience of tourists...that was tough for me to hear in the November Hawaii daylight.

"Do you know why I put my clothes inside out?" I asked reluctantly.

"You told us Fred wanted to do a fashion show."

Finally, it clicked. Fred *is* my gay ghost. He was with me as a teen ensuring I saw *9 to 5*, during the college years to signify the importance of *Steel Magnolias*, in my twenties when I needed to be reminded of *Flashdance*, in my thirties to highlight *Moonstruck*, and now to spotlight a legendary Diana Ross/Lionel Richie song and the elation of a spontaneous fashion show. He visits me on Halloween to enjoy the gay '80s pop culture touchstones. My best guess is that he passed away in the decade and his unfinished business is teaching younger homosexuals about the pertinent stuff, knowing that as a '90s kid, I am not *as* familiar with the classics of the decade I was born. I'm grateful to Fred for acting as my spirit guide and showing me a good time, ensuring I am familiar with the queens who came before my time.

Some monsters appear when it's a full moon, the Sanderson sisters come out to play when a virgin lights a black-flame candle, and Fred arrives on Halloween night to relive the queerest parts of the Reagan decade. For all of you out there who are skeptical of the supernatural, I encourage you to keep an eye out this October 31 for your own gay ghost because there's nothing more magical than a night out with a homosexual who has an affinity for the film work of Dolly Parton.

Author's Note: In writing this chapter, I realized that in each instance when I thought I was visited by a gay ghost named Fred, I had been not just drinking but drinking something called absinthe, a hallucinogenic liquor that may or may not have been the reason I thought I was being chased by a homosexual spirit. Oops. Drink responsibly next Halloween.

Halloween Costume Idea:

If you're a rom-com lover like me, perhaps consider turning your favorite heroines into zombies. Zombie Meryl from *It's Complicated*, zombie Kate Hudson from *How to Lose a Guy in 10 Days*, or even zombie Queen Latifah from *Last Holiday*. A little makeup goes a long way! Here I am dressed as zombie Diane Keaton from *Something's Gotta Give* on Halloween 2015 for inspiration:

The Strand

The winter sun falls sooner than the day before as I reach for a loaded shoebox tucked away in a closet behind extra rolls of double ply. Wrapped in an old newspaper is a strand of holiday lights. They aren't the reds and greens I bought at the store two years ago or the twinkle lights I got on clearance last January 23. They're the kitschy Looney Tunes lights from when I was seven.

It's hard to remember where I got them, but I can still smell the perfume Mom wore when she helped me hang them in my childhood bedroom. I remember her tucking me into bed, then gently rubbing my forehead as my eyelids grew heavy and the lights grew dim. She quietly unplugged the strand before leaving my room. I can hear the coffeepot growling from the kitchen as I drifted to sleep. Dad poured Mom a cup to share in hopes that it would keep them both awake long enough to wrap presents and mark them *from Santa* before hiding them in places they sometimes couldn't remember come Christmas Eve. Dad always stayed up about an hour less than Mom.

I remember the next morning; I woke up late on my first day of winter break. It was the day my dog chewed off three of the lights. I'd have stopped her if I weren't busy building snow castles with my brothers in the front yard. Mom and Dad were inside doing parent things—baking and cleaning, napping and organizing. Our faces were red, and our feet were cold, despite being wrapped in old shopping bags and snow boots, but my brothers and I went inside as soon as it got dark, and I again lit my bedroom with the now-three-fewer strand.

I unwrap and untangle them now as an adult, and the memories of that time come rushing back to me at the speed of twinkling light. I can hear my old dog barking and the grunt of my dad's familiar snore on the brown sofa we had two years too long. I can smell the butterball cookies my mom had in the oven, nutty and rolled in powdered sugar, a recipe passed down from her mom, and if I close my eyes, I can see my brothers, who are now men, as boys, one with oversize glasses and the other with the crooked nose he earned from a middle school basketball game.

It's now my first Christmas without my family, and I wish the tears could numb the sadness that fills my heart when I reach for that dusty old shoebox. Instead, the tears fall on the bulbs, and I use the vintage paper to wipe them dry. It makes the strand look shiny and new for a split second, but then I see the place where my dog chewed, and I plug them in and notice the three that are still out all these years later. The memories escape as the tears dry and the lights flicker. I breathe in and try to hold on to the smells, the sights, the sounds elicited by the strand, wishing I could have my loved ones near me again in more than just a memory that fades each year.

Pain barges through the door, often unexpectedly, destroying everything in its path while you try to catch your footing and kick it out. Heartbreak, though, it taps quietly on the door, sneaks in when you're not paying close enough attention, and infects your surroundings. It leaves you off-balance, dizzy, and unable to process what's happening until it's already too late. A broken heart can be put back together, but it's never the same. The heartbreak is here now, and I'll never be the same. I can't fix it or kick it out. I can only coexist.

I proudly hang my childhood lights on a side table, and although they look cheap and worn next to the modern decor, I don't care. I don't care that they don't shine boldly like they used to or that they don't match the other bright white lights on my fake tree. I don't care that I'm attaching such importance to some item that sits idle in the back of a closet for eleven months out of the year. I don't care because when I need my loved ones and they're not close enough for me to hug, plugging in the strand is the next best thing.

The Nativity

The year was 1992. First grade. Catholic school. My class was putting on a holiday play, something to do with Mary, Joseph, and the inn they got booted from. From a very young age, I was taught the story of Jesus's birth, the three wise men, a star, etc. I can't say I relate to Jesus's heterosexual parents' Christmas experience because I'm gay and the only time I've ever been kicked out of an establishment is when I went to a Shania Twain concert in Las Vegas. (An usher said I had too much to drink, and apparently some of the other patrons complained that I was singing "Man, I Feel Like a Woman" too loudly. *That* was blasphemous.) Regardless, I've never been turned away from lodging, so I'm sure it's especially tough when you've been traveling by foot or camel and you're preggers. The religious tale, a holiday staple, was repeated to me every year since my own birth, and when I was seven years old, my schoolteacher thought it would be appropriate for us to recreate the legendary Christmas night as a performance for our parents.

The story of Mary and Joseph doesn't have a ton of characters for students to play in an adaptation. *Ocean's Eleven* might've worked better, but that wasn't in the cards for Saint Rita Elementary. Instead, the teacher cast the few main roles while assigning most of my peers as horses, camels, sheep, and other randos that were added to the script to accommodate over thirty children. I remember one kid was dressed as a black cat for the nativity play because his mom had a leftover costume from Halloween that she insisted they let him use. Our teacher, already mentally on winter break, gave in, and suddenly a cat was listed in the playbill. The play narrator had to explain that the cat followed Mother Mary from Nazareth so that the audience would understand why a young boy named Christopher was purring in the background of every scene. The program credited him as Chris the Christmas Cat and confused a lot of us. So much holiday imagery is thrown at young people, and they're expected to understand how Jesus and Santa are both somehow the leading men of Christmas. Now here comes a cat named Chris, leading many young impressionable students to deduce that the Christmas holiday might've been named after the character, the only student whose recently divorced mother, Marnie, refused to spend any extra money at Joann Fabric for a costume she knew would only be worn once. Marnie had legal bills to pay and a fresh perm waiting.

Fortunately, I didn't have to play an animal. Instead, I got to portray an angel, specifically the angel narrator! I was the first one the audience saw, and I got to explain the cat situation. It wasn't a lead role exactly, but it had more lines than the man and woman who ran the inn. If this was *Ocean's Eleven*, then I was Matt Damon—not the lead but also not Scott Caan. My job was to welcome everyone to the show, introduce the first scene and our cast of characters, and then step aside until the end when I'd shoo baby Jesus and the cat off the stage to say goodbye to the audience.

I took my responsibilities very seriously, as I've always wanted to be an entertainer. I daydreamed about a modeling scout being in the audience, sweeping me away to Hollywood to make me a star. Not only did I have to know my lines, but I had to look great too. As soon as I booked the role, I rushed home to tell my mom that I needed to look like the best angel the town had ever seen! Linda Pellegrino can do a lot of things, and she's the greatest woman on planet earth, but she's not super crafty. She can cook the best casserole you'll ever have, but she's not great with a hot glue gun. Being that we were also living on a tight budget back then, it meant my costume was simply going to be one of my mom's white button-down shirts. We planned on using my dad's shirt, but the morning of the show, he saw his shirt pressed and thought it meant he was supposed to wear it to work. Mom improvised and ironed her ladies' business wear instead. When I told her I needed a halo, she told me to "figure it out," so I went to my teacher, who tossed me a left-over pipe cleaner. Since my costume was shit, I knew I'd have to dazzle with my performance. I'd studied my lines, changed a few words in the script to play to my strengths, left room for improvisation, and learned to project my voice so it would carry to the back of the room. I basically just shouted every word during rehearsal, in an acting style multiple teachers back then and throughout my adult life describe as "too loud," but that's neither here nor there.

The final and only performance was the last day of school before winter break. We were supposed to arrive at the classroom in the morning, get into costume for one last rehearsal, have a quick lunch in the cafeteria, and at *exactly* one o'clock, our audience (parents who either didn't work or were able to get off work) would enjoy the fruits of our labor. After the show, the kids and their guests would have a party, which mostly meant snowflake-shaped Jell-O and Hi-C juice boxes. Mom sent me off on the school bus that morning with a kiss, ensuring me that although Dad and my grandparents were booked for the day, she would be leaving work early to come see my big play. She also told me to be careful with her shirt. I was elated.

Dress rehearsal was perfect—some might even say Meryl-esque—and the confidence it gave me turned me into a monster. I walked around the cafeteria encouraging the young lady playing Mary to enunciate, told Joseph his costume made him look hunchbacked when he didn't elongate his neck, and even asked Chris the Christmas Cat to be more aware of his entrances. Like Tom Cruise on the *War of the Worlds* press tour, I was a nightmare. Lunch wrapped up, and we all headed back to the theater (a classroom with the desks removed) for the big performance. As the guests flooded in, I was walking on cloud nine, excited to show off my skills to my mom. I figured if a modeling scout wasn't in the audience, Mom would at least recognize my talents and whisk me away to the West Coast to become a star—my own Midwest Dina Lohan.

More and more people arrived as the clock got closer to one. I saw my friend Brian's mom, my buddy Michael's grandparents, and even a girl named Kelly's older brother, a sixth grader who got special permission to come watch the show. It felt like absolutely everyone was there...except Linda Pellegrino. Mom was a busy woman, but she *always* showed up. If for some reason she couldn't make it to an event, she would send my dad, a grandparent, or an aunt in her place. Someone would be there because someone was always there. By quarter after one, the flop sweat started, and there was still no sign of anyone from my circle. My teacher asked me if I was ready. WAS I READY? Of course not! Mom wasn't there! Dreams of becoming Hollywood royalty were slipping by, and furthermore, I couldn't possibly perform without emotional support in the audience.

"We need to begin," my teacher proclaimed. "The guests are getting antsy."

I froze, and within moments, I did what I assume Nicole Kidman does before a take when she doesn't have a handle on whatever accent she's attempting...I cried. And I cried. And I cried some more. Again, this show was being done in a classroom, not in a theater, so I wasn't behind a curtain; I was simply sobbing in front of the crowded room. The audience awkwardly stared while the other students reveled in my misery. I had just spent an entire lunch hour telling them all how glib they were as actors, and now I couldn't even start the show. As if that weren't bad enough, they couldn't begin without me because I opened the whole shebang! It wouldn't make sense without my angel character explaining why there was a fucking cat onstage for the nativity. How would the audience know why there were seven wise men traveling on Christmas Eve instead of the traditional three? And what would the crowd make of them carrying not frankincense, gold, and myrrh but a leftover Jell-O snowflake and a handful of pencil erasers since one of the other students had vomited on some of the props? (He forgot his lunch, and the staff ran out of whatever they were cooking, so he had to have a leftover meal. The lunch lady called it Salisbury steak, but was it maybe dog food? Unclear.)

The teacher told me we could wait until 1:30, half an hour later than planned, but then the show had to start because she was planning on going home early, and pushing it back any further meant she wouldn't be there by four to watch *Oprah*.

1:28 p.m.: Still no Mom.

1:29 p.m.: The door opened, and I thought maybe it was my mom, but instead it was the lunch lady tiptoeing in to either watch the show or apologize to the young boy she'd poisoned an hour earlier.

1:30 p.m.: Time to start the show!

My teacher walked toward me, and I knew what was

coming. She was going to tell me the show must go on. The conversation went something like this (probably)...

"Are you okay to go on, or do you want me to do your part?" the teacher asked me gently.

"How dare you put me between a rock and a hard place? Please just give me ten more minutes!"

"There's no time! You get your ass out there and start the fucking nativity play, or I will!"

"You want to throw the fucks around? I'll throw the fucks around! I am not starting the *fucking* play until my *fucking* mother is in the *fucking* audience. You fucking got that?" I replied, wide-eyed and firm.

"That's it. I'm going out there and reading your lines!"

"You bitch."

The teacher began exiting to the front of the stage.

"No, wait! I'll fucking go," I said.

I walked in front of the audience, tears still streaming from my eyes, no strength to deliver my lines with any oomph after I just wasted my energy on the impatient instructor. I mumbled through the script, barely enunciating, like an early Gerard Butler performance. Inside, I was a mess. As soon as I was done with the intro, I ran out of the classroom to get some space and calm my nerves. There was no way I could stay inside and see all the proud parents watching their kids play absurd animals. And the last thing I wanted to see in that moment was a Halloween cat meowing through the birth of Christ.

There I was, in the hallway of my grade school, sitting with my knees to my chest and thinking about how mad I was at my mother. How could she do this to me? She never did this to me! I wish I could say I was worried about her, but the truth is, at that age, you think everyone around you is invincible. The thought that something had happened to her didn't even cross my mind. *She must've decided not to come.* Just as my tears started to mix with the anger, I heard a bell and saw my mom running down the hall in a red blazer (complete with shoulder pads because it was the early '90s). Around her neck was a beaded green-and-red necklace I had made her the year before as a gift, complete with a bell in the center. I looked up and saw Mom, her eyes matching mine: filled with tears.

"I missed it." She sighed as she sat on the cold cracked tile next to me, knees to her chest.

"You missed it," I replied.

"Danster, I'm sorry. Someone rear-ended my car, and they insisted we report it even though there was no damage. I did everything I could," she explained.

I wish I could say I forgave her immediately, understanding that accidents happen and sometimes life is out of your control. Instead, I seethed with anger, unable to control my emotions. She'd let me down.

Shortly thereafter, the play ended. I never went back inside the room, but the other students did join me in the hallway, where the holiday party was set to begin now that the nativity theater performance was done. Some of the other PTA parents passed out candy and festively shaped Jell-O, while a mom with a camera offered to snap photos of the kids with their guests. When she approached us, Mom insisted that we smile for the photo. A Christmas memory we could cherish forever, she thought. Problem is, I didn't want to smile. The result is a photo that makes me look like a child warlock in an oversize ladies' shirt.

Mom faked the best smile she could when she gripped my shoulders to pose for the Polaroid. The photo made its way to a Popsicle stick picture frame with a red-and-green ribbon tied at the top, which we hooked on our tree each December. Year after year, Mom and I would decorate the tree with a collection of homemade ornaments. We would hang the memory on a branch and reminisce about that day at school. Eventually, I moved out of the house, and Mom would give me a call around Thanksgiving, after she trimmed the family tree, to remind me just how badly she wanted to be there for me that day in grade school.

Now that I'm an adult, I have my own box of ornaments to hang. As I get the decorations out of storage, I think about how lucky I am. Although I wish Mom could've seen me perform that day, I am grateful she desperately wanted to be there. No adult wants to sit through a first-grade play—hell, most adults don't want to sit through *any* play. But she did.

When I visit my parents' house and see that familiar Popsicle-stick ornament on their large fake tree, I don't remember the sadness I felt in the first grade, the first time I realized my mom wasn't invincible. What sticks out now is the sound of the bell shaking as she rushed toward me in the school hallway. Her beautiful brown eyes that were passed down to me filled with tears, just like mine. I no longer care that she didn't make it. I'm simply thankful I had a mom I wanted to be there more than anything and that she felt the same. The holiday season is not about the gifts or the decorations; it's about the people you'll do anything to see.

Cookie Cutters

THE FANCY GROCERY STORES ARE ROBBING US EVERY CHRISTMAS, AND IT HAS TO STOP.

I have the fondest memories of making cutout cookies with Mom in early December, rolling out the dough onto a floured surface, pressing the tree-shaped cutter into the mix, and carefully lifting the dough off the counter and onto a baking sheet. The cookies would either be in the shapes of trees from the cutter or round balls that my mom said were snowflakes (even though they were simply round blobs). The treats would come out of the oven, and we'd wait for them to cool before topping them with vanilla icing and red and green sprinkles. That was it—ready to serve.

That tree cookie cutter we used was passed down over generations. As I got older and started going into nicer grocery stores and markets, I learned about the sham business that is the cookie cutter industry. IT MUST STOP. I *love* making food into shapes. Trust me, there is nothing more fulfilling than seeing your dough turn into a cute little decoration, but those ornate cutters are absolute shit. We are being hoodwinked!

For one thing, the cookie usually expands in the oven, so those tiny cutters end up making something that looks shapeless anyway. I recently bought a Chip and Joanna cookie cutter from their collection, and it was supposed to make cookies in the shape of a house. I'd binged three seasons of *Fixer Upper* (more on this later) right before going to the store, so I was hypnotized by my love of the show into getting the cookie cutter. It barely makes any fucking sense. Why would I want to serve someone that for the holidays? A farmhouse? I suppose you could make little home cookies for an open house if you were a real estate agent, but we're stretching the definition of *festive* here.

That's not even the craziest one I've seen. Williams-Sonoma once tricked me into purchasing a Grinch cookie cutter set, yet none of my cookies ended up looking like Cindy Lou Who, Max the Dog, or Jim Carrey when he terrorized people on the set of the live-action version of *How the Grinch Stole Christmas*. They all came out of the oven looking like crap. Now I know some of you are reading this and thinking that it's my fault, that I'm using a cookie recipe that needs to be altered to fit cutout cookies, but I promise you that's not it. The Grinch baking set is so ornate that you need to be Picasso to make something that resembles Cindy Lou Who. By the way, have you seen Cindy Lou Who? When Ron Howard made the Grinch movie, the actors spent *hours* in hair and makeup so they could look like the characters in the book. Producers literally had to hire a CIA agent trained in torture endurance to help Jim Carrey get into his insane costume. How the hell can I be expected to make my cookies look even remotely like that?

At least the Grinch cutters are great for fans of the movie. Memorabilia, if you will. I've seen upscale markets sell way more absurd shapes. I've seen owls, face masks, and even a cat's ass. That's right, a shop nearby was selling a cookie cutter that was in the shape of a cat's bare ass, with a tail that went up. I'm not even sure I'm properly explaining it, but picture a cat's ass, and that's what it was. For Christmas!

"You're selling this cookie cutter of a cat's ass, why?" I asked the salesclerk.

"For Christmas cookies."

"What does a cat's ass have to do with the season?" I asked.

She had no answer for me. Did you ever watch *Dawson's Creek* on streaming before they got the rights to air the iconic Paula Cole opening credit music? The theme song they replaced it with was odd and ruined the whole vibe of the show because it just didn't fit with the adventures of Dawson, Pacey, Joey, Jen, and Grams. The cat's ass cookie cutter just didn't fit with Christmas! Maybe the cookie cutter makers saw my elementary school nativity play and decided to build a shape based off the cat?

To anyone out there who makes seasonal cookies with a cat's bare ass, please reach out and let me know what kind of sprinkles you use to finish them off. Also, if my cookies look too good to be homemade this year, that's because I gave up and bought some from the store. Don't tell anyone.

Now and Then

When's the last time you bought yourself a gift? If you're anything like me, you overthink every purchase until all the fun is sucked out of the entire process. Even something as simple as a muffin is debated ad nauseam in my head if unplanned. I stumble into a coffee shop, see a treat, and overthink it. *Do I need to spend the money? Is this going to ruin my diet? Do I have something like it already at home?* These are all valid questions, things to be considered before spending hard-earned cash, but occasionally, I wish I could live with financial abandon, treating myself to something, anything, even if its pleasures are fleeting. Every time I was forbidden something as a kid, I'd think about how things would be different when I was in charge, when I was older and had my own money, but things aren't any different. I've replaced my parents' denial with my own. I've never been able to spend recklessly, which should be a good thing, but it endlessly frustrates me when I'm trying to be footloose and fancy-free. Since I struggle with purchasing something unplanned, I decided I would *plan* to buy myself a Christmas gift last year. Something no one else would know about, something just for me, an enchanting gift that, at first, I didn't know how much I needed.

Most '80s and '90s kids probably remember the Scholastic Book Fair. It was a magical time in elementary school when students would gather around books and posters and fancy erasers that were way too costly. Ten-year-olds would browse the boutique in the school gymnasium with whatever money they had saved (or that their parents would give them). In between those quarterly pop-up shops, teachers would pass out thin paper catalogs with an order form attached. It was pre-Amazon. You would take home the catalog, browse for hours with a pen, circle the Animorphs or Baby-Sitters Club books you wanted, then beg Mom or Dad to provide the funds to help you acquire these items. If the cash was collected, you would turn in the order form; the ordered items would be delivered to school a couple of weeks later and passed out to the class. The wealthy kids would gather their loot, while others went home empty-handed, unable to secure the bag and get their goods. Around November, the *holiday* Scholastic catalog would be released, and each November, I was obsessed!

Seasonal versions of favorite book series would be featured, like the Goosebumps book about the evil snowman, or ornament arts and crafts kits. I particularly gravitated to the movie tie-ins. These were book versions of the hot kid movies of the year, essentially the script broken into chapters, with full-color photos from the set sandwiched in. They also did this with TV shows, so you could buy *Full House* chapter books based on Stephanie Tanner alongside a paperback version of *Flubber*.

Which brings me to 1996, when a film became available on VHS that forever changed me. A pivotal piece of pop culture that will never be forgotten. That film was *Now and Then*. A moderate hit when it was released in theaters the previous year, *Now and Then* flourished when it was finally on home video. For the unfamiliar, it's a coming-of-age story starring four young women (Gaby Hoffmann, Christina Ricci, Thora Birch, and the late Ashleigh Aston Moore) as preteens living, laughing, loving (and performing séances) during a significant 1970s summer in the Midwest. We also spend time with the adult versions of the characters, played wonderfully by Demi Moore (who also produced), Rosie O'Donnell, Melanie Griffith, and Rita Wilson in the present day. There were plenty of great movies (like *Stand by Me*) about young boys entering their teen years, but rarely, if ever, were these stories centered on girls.

Every young woman at my school wanted to see this movie. And they did! I so badly wanted to head to the theater with them to watch what was surely the cinema event of the century, but unfortunately, I was too self-conscious about my interests. Growing up with no sisters, only two very masculine older brothers who loved *The Karate Kid* and *The Terminator*, I struggled to embrace my pop culture interests that often skewed feminine. Occasionally, I would get lucky: Mom would rent *The First Wives Club* and I'd get to watch with her, or my older brother's girlfriend would check out whatever Julia Roberts was doing from the local library, and I'd watch before they returned it, but usually, I had to wait until cable to catch the chick flicks. When *Now and Then* was released on VHS, I had to see it! I saved up my coins, and as soon as it became a dollar rental at my local video store, I ran inside while my mom was at the grocery store next door and rented it alongside more masculine movies so no one would know.

"What'd you get?" Mom asked.

"Just that *Three Ninjas* movie and the sequel," I lied.

That first viewing of *Now and Then* was magical. I related to Teeny's love of Hollywood, understood Chrissy's naivete, felt a kinship with Samantha because she always had a book in her hands, and envied Roberta getting her first kiss! I dreamed of sitting around with friends, taking magazine quizzes, running into Janeane Garofalo, and riding bikes in the neighborhood with my besties.

The other girls in my class would come in Monday morning and talk about their slumber parties, how they stayed up late watching *Now and Then.* I wanted to join their conversations, tell them how I most identified with Roberta, and share details of our mutual crush on Devon Sawa. I just wasn't strong enough to do so. I held my love inside after I returned my rental to the drop box.

When that November holiday Scholastic catalog came, I scrolled through the pages and saw something beautiful listed alongside *Merry Christmas, Amelia Bedelia,* and *Garfield's Christmas Tales.* It was the movie tie-in book for *Now and Then.*

The cover was pink and featured a picture of the entire female cast. The tagline ("In every woman is the girl she left behind") was printed on the front in bold letters. It was unapologetically marketed toward girls, and I *had* to have it. Since I wasn't secure enough to ask for the VHS from Santa, this was the next best thing. I devised a plan to get the book version without much damage to my reputation. Mom wouldn't always let me get books, but the holiday Scholastic catalog was different. She'd give me ten or fifteen dollars as an end-of-the-year treat.

The plan: I'd get the cash or check and tell Mom it was for Goosebumps, then check the box next to *Now and Then* on the order form. When the books arrived at the classroom, the teacher would hand me my item, and I'd feign resistance, insisting it was a mix-up at HQ if any of the other students questioned why I bought the girliest book ever published. It was foolproof. I fantasized about sitting by my Christmas tree, reading about the adventures of my four new favorite gals. It would be my little secret.

The box came to my fifth-grade classroom on the last day of school before holiday break, and it felt like Christmas morning. Watching a teacher unbox a bunch of brand-new books from Scholastic was way better than any PR unboxing I've ever seen on IG. I waited impatiently for my teacher to hand me my copy. One by one, she would pass out everyone's gifts during the scheduled silent-reading time. Although the books came with a giant piece of paper taped on top indicating the student's name and order number, making it hard to tell what the item was, and no one was supposed to be talking, I still planned what I would say if anyone spotted my haul.

They sent me the wrong book, ugh! I would scream before stuffing my pink book into my boy-blue backpack.

Finally, my moment came.

"Danny, here's your order..."

I ran to the teacher's desk and ripped off the receipt only to find...

A biography about fish. They sent me the wrong book! I WAS LIVID.

"Excuse me, this isn't what I ordered."

"Hm, let me see if I have the original order form in here."

My fifth-grade teacher rustled through the box, passing copy after copy of *Now and Then* that the girls in class had ordered.

"I'm sorry. I don't have the original order forms. You sure you didn't accidentally mark that you wanted the fish book? Sometimes things get mixed up," she said.

Of course I was sure! I had never been more fucking sure of anything in my entire fucking life! I WANTED MY *NOW AND THEN* BOOK! I needed to see the production photos of Demi and Gaby on set! Surely one of those copies in the box was mine, but I didn't have the confidence to ask for it. Instead, I defeatedly took my stupid fish book and sat my gay ass back down. My lady peers spent the rest of silent reading hour immersed in their pink books, while I spent my final hours before winter break reading about eels. Holiday ruined.

When the January Scholastic catalog came around, the pink copy of the movie book was gone, not even an ordering option! My chance at getting it vanished. Pretty soon, the movie started playing on cable, and we had a VCR that recorded, so one day when I was left home alone, I grabbed one of my mom's old *All My Children* tapes and recorded the Christina Ricci classic over Erica Kane and company. It was the next best thing. The picture was blurry, and often Kelly Ripa and Mark Consuelos as Hayley and Mateo would interject, but it was otherwise perfect. I'd rewatch any time I wanted when no one was around to see.

Last Christmas, as a grown-ish man, I thought about my quest for the *Now and Then* book. I'm so comfortable in my own skin now that I look back with sympathy at that scared little boy who was afraid to ask for a simple book he wanted, worried he would be shamed for liking something meant for his female peers. I decided it would be the gift I bought myself. My planned treat.

Laptop in hand, I was scrolling the internet when my boyfriend came in the room.

"Anything you want for Christmas this year?"

"There is one thing, but I'm just gonna buy it for myself."

I navigated my browser to eBay, where I searched for the *Now and Then* book. There was a copy available for $6.13 with my name on it. The internet is a wondrous place.

The paperback arrived a week later with a few tears and pen markings throughout the pages, a faded cover, and what looked like a coffee stain on the back, but it was perfect. Like the characters who spent the movie reminiscing about their childhood, I spent that afternoon looking back on mine. I felt so proud to have built a life my childhood self could be happy about, one he could only dream was possible. A life where I'm not afraid to embrace the things that make me *me*. When my significant other asked me what I wanted for Christmas, I wasn't ashamed to ask him for it; I simply wanted to treat my younger self. I still haven't read the book, but it sits on my bookshelf as a reminder of the insecure little boy I left behind.

Buy yourself a present this year. And if you don't know what to get, order something for the child you left behind.

Knives Out

Everyone does Turkey Day a little differently. I love seeing the many ways people prepare their meals, the various cultural traditions people use to show their love. My favorite part is always the stuffing (a.k.a. dressing), which to me means white bread, lots of butter, spices, eggs, onions, celery, and love. I learned that I need to always bring my own no matter where I'm headed; otherwise, I'm destined for disappointment. A friend once served me stuffing with grapes and mushrooms in it, and—I say this with love—THEY DESERVE JAIL TIME. Usually, people crave whatever they grew up with, the nostalgia influencing our tastes buds, so if you're someone whose mother served Pillsbury crescent rolls when you were seven, chances are you're leaving room on your plate for one at thirty-five too.

I was around twenty-four when I stopped regularly doing the Pellegrino family Thanksgiving. It was too expensive and troublesome to travel from California to Ohio at the end of November *and* the end of December, so I often chose Christmas. I'd do Friendsgiving instead, or I'd be someone's plus-one to their childhood homes. It was always amazing to me that regardless of the family background of the home I was going into, there was always a constant: the person cooking the main dish was always, without fail, on the brink of a breakdown, and I've never once witnessed anything quite like the Thanksgiving 2012 breakdown at the Fritz residence.

My invite to the Fritz household came courtesy of my buddy Eric, who knew the youngest Fritz daughter, Denise, from work. They weren't super close, but Denise was looking for new friends, and Eric and I both found ourselves solo for the holiday. The Fritz family was stationed in Southern California, which is rare. It feels like all of California is filled with transplants from other places, but there are a lot of beautiful suburban areas around Los Angeles loaded with people who grew up here. Tucked away in Thousand Oaks, the Fritz fam lived in a cozy cul-de-sac—filled with nearly identical luxe houses—that looked straight out of *Desperate Housewives*. They were McMansions, the only difference in each being the color of paint slathered on the outside.

Eric and I pulled up to the Fritz house and immediately noticed the next-door neighbor's house stood out in that the lawn was covered in decor. At first, it was hard to tell what was on the grass, but as we got closer, it became clear: holiday inflatables. If you've ever been to Walmart or Target between the months of October and December, you know the ones

I'm talking about. The giant, blow-up snowmen, snow globes, trees, and Santas that go in the yard. They're aggressive to the eye when they are fully erect, but when they aren't, they look like cartoons who were flattened by anvils. There's something dark and depressing about these lawn ornaments when they aren't filled with air. But the only thing more depressing is when they *are* filled and greeting people on the street. I *love* decorations, but I find these so..."look at me." Perhaps some of you adorn your lawns with these, and I'm sorry to be the one to tell you this, but they're ugly and impersonal. Go get some vintage plastic Santas, or stick with classic lights. Anything but the yard balloons. In this case, the yard had a giant turkey wearing a pilgrim hat.

Eric and I entered the Fritz house and were immediately greeted by the matriarch, Janeane Fritz, who came at us with a smile that can only be described as morning Valium mixed with cooking wine, the traditional Thanksgiving cocktail of all at-home chefs getting ready for a family meal.

"Did you see those fucking ugly decorations next door? Don't even get me started," Janeane said before even a *hello* or a *nice to meet you*.

Keep in mind, I had never said two words to this woman before, and I barely even knew her daughter. In fact, Eric and I probably should've declined the invitation as we were all essentially strangers. Only now we were strangers on a team together, ones who shared a collective enemy in the tacky next-door neighbors.

"Those inflatables? Ugh, yes, they can't even loosen the purse strings enough to keep them blown up on a holiday? They're just flat on the grass," I said, sucking up to Janeane with my judgment.

"Are you serious? I thought they had them blown up today. They're such trash, that Mitzy and Dave," Janeane said. "Shit, I better get back to the kitchen. Welcome to our home."

Denise came to the doorway to take our jackets and introduced us to the rest of the group while Janeane went back in.

Eric buddied up with some guy named Sam who he thought was gay but was also maybe married to Denise's cousin Shelly? We're not sure. Eric always had a knack for sleeping with straight guys, so his holiday mission was set, while I did what I do best:

I found the oldest breathing woman to cozy up to for the day. This meant Grandma Jojo, who unfortunately proved to be a bit *too* old for me. Don't get me wrong, I still poured myself a giant glass of pinot grigio and sat my ass next to her, but she wasn't quite with it. Her sister, Aunt Wendy, was only slightly younger, but she kept trying to talk to me about politics, and I didn't have the patience. Once I realized Grandma J. was close to death (and attempting to converse with the dog) and Aunt Wendy was canvassing for Trump, I walked my butt into the kitchen to chat with Janeane. I was Goldilocks, and Janeane was just right when it came to women over sixty for me to befriend for the day.

Maybe it's the gay thing, but women between the age of forty and whatever Grandma Jojo was tend to open up to me in ways I can't quite explain.

"Did you meet my lazy fucking husband, David?" Janeane asked as if we were the oldest of friends. I can't imagine she talked that way to other strangers, but it's always been my superpower. Even as a young boy, I would befriend the moms at slumber parties instead of socializing with my peers. They would tell me their troubles, and I would listen.

"No, I don't think I've met him. Can I help you with anything?" I asked, offering to change the subject in case she wanted to ease into conversation about her husband.

"He's probably sleeping in the basement, that dumb shit," she replied.

I like a swearer, but even I was feeling like Janeane was filled with a little too much hostility.

"Guys can be so useless sometimes. Should I pour you a glass of wine?" I asked, hoping to relieve some tension by agreeing with her and offering a solution (booze).

"God bless you, yes, I'll have a tall glass of anything."

I went over to the makeshift bar on the kitchen counter and poured Janeane some of the pinot noir I recognized. It was an eighteen-dollar bottle, which I thought was classy at the time, when in fact it was probably the cheapest bottle there, likely brought by Cousin Shelly, whom I later found out was left out of the inheritance when the patriarch passed.

"David! Can you come help me?" Janeane shouted into the ether. It wasn't even directed anywhere, just sent to the high heavens as she mixed some gravy and placed some dinner rolls on a baking sheet.

"He's a fucking asshole. Piece of shit," she said under her breath about her husband of over forty years.

"I'm happy to help," I offered.

"That is sweet, but I need him to get *OFF HIS LAZY ASS* and get the napkins from the back of my car," she said.

Not a peep came from David. I assume he was either asleep or dodging his wife, who was now chugging the wine I put in front of her.

"Fill me up, Cookie," she said, surely forgetting my name and instead deciding to call me *Cookie* as if she were Harvey Fierstein and I were a chorus boy in *Hairspray*.

I poured her more wine while she tended to the food. Janeane mixed mashed potatoes, heated up corn, and melted marshmallows on the most delicious-looking sweet potato casserole I've ever seen, all the while balancing her wine. But the more she drank, the more vulgar Janeane became.

"Fucking turkey holiday and my fucking dumb shit husband can't get his goddamn ass up to help me. I cook for his asshole mother. Goddamn piece of shit..." she mumbled to herself. You know how Joe Pesci mumbles obscenities in *Home Alone* when his hair is lit on fire or he trips on ice? Janeane was like that, only using actual swear words instead of whatever Joe had to say to keep a PG rating.

"What a dumb shit," she added. In fact, she kept calling him a dumb shit. It was her go-to insult.

Being that she had knives and fire nearby, I decided to be as nice as humanly possible and hopefully stay on her good side. Her wrath knew no bounds. When David finally stumbled into the kitchen, hair a mess and seemingly still half asleep from a nap, Janeane ordered him to retrieve her precious napkins in the car.

"Janeane, let me go change really quick. I didn't realize company was already here. I'll get the napkins after I do," David said as he stumbled to his bedroom to remove his *Family Guy* T-shirt without even saying *hello*.

I looked around to see if other people were seeing what I was seeing—something way more compelling than any of the scenes from *Marriage Story*. Adam Driver and Scarlett Johansson had *nothing* on Janeane and David. Unfortunately, everyone else was missing the show. Eric and his maybe-straight crush were lost in each other's eyes, while Shelly started a card game with Denise. Aunt Wendy was knee-deep in cable news, and Grandma Jojo was likely immune to the feud. At ninety, her eyes had already seen all there is to see when it comes to domestic partnerships. Her husband passed years earlier, so she had time to relive all the good times and bad in her mind. I also think maybe she thought the dog was her husband? Anyway...

Janeane moved on to the turkey, deciding she was going to carve the bird and plate it while her husband changed. She gripped her carving knife and giant fork, only pausing her mission to drink more wine. I knew David would be back soon, so to stay close to the action, I offered to make a charcuterie plate from the meats and cheeses she had in the refrigerator. I slowly layered cheese and crackers while Janeane fumed about having to do most of the work for this shindig.

"Denise! Can you help us in the kitchen?" she asked.

"I'm playing cards!" Denise replied.

Janeane's eyes went wide, and she took another chug of wine, seemingly the only thing keeping her from having an aneurysm right then and there.

"Fucking lazy-ass motherfucking family can't do one goddamn thing for me," she said as she pierced the cooked meat with the fire of a thousand suns.

David finally came downstairs. "Okay, I'm changed. What do you need?"

"I need you to get the fucking napkins I asked you to get me a thousand fucking times already, dumb shit," Janeane said.

David's eyes darted toward the empty wineglass near Janeane's right hand.

"Are you drinking?" he asked.

"Yes, I needed a fucking drink," she replied.

"Fuck, Janeane, you're ruining your sobriety for this?"

😮!

Uh-oh. I never got clarity on how long she had been sober, but I was the one who poured her the first drink, and David seemed completely in shock that she was back on the sauce.

"I'm sorry, I didn't know—" I said apologetically.

"Mom, you're drinking again?" Denise said as she walked into the kitchen, tears forming in her eyes.

"Maybe if I got some fucking help! Where are my fucking napkins?" Janeane shouted to take the attention away from her boozing.

It was pure chaos. Denise and David were finally upright and in the kitchen, but clearly a family trauma had been unleashed. Eric, meanwhile, was fully hand-on-knee with Denise's cousin's husband. Shelly had noticed Eric flirting and told her husband to stop it as if he were a dog humping a pillow. I stood in shock at the events unfolding around me.

"I'll get the napkins my-fucking-self," Janeane said as she grabbed the car keys from the nearby counter.

Not knowing what else to do, I simply ran to the front door and held it open for Janeane to walk through. She stomped by me in a huff and immediately looked to her right. Mitzy, the next-door neighbor, had finally inflated her lawn decor.

"Are you fucking kidding me?" Janeane said to herself as she turned back around and went into the kitchen. "Keep holding that door for me!" she said.

Janeane grabbed the carving knife she had been using for the bird in her right hand, car keys still gripped in her left. She shot past me and into the yard next door. Janeane took her knife and began stabbing the inflatable turkey with intensity, as if she were Michael Myers in *Halloween* or Mike Myers trying to cut himself out of prosthetics after wrapping *The Cat in the Hat*. The decorative balloon flattened while Janeane made her way to the driveway and dug the autumnal napkins out of the trunk of their family car.

The air was also taken out of the metaphorical balloon inside the house. David and Denise fell in line, finally contributing by setting the table. Eric formed a truce with Shelly, Aunt Wendy turned off Tucker Carlson, and Grandma Jojo wheeled herself to the dinner table, unfazed by all of it. We proceeded to say grace as if nothing had happened, like Janeane never broke her sobriety or destroyed her neighbor's ugly lawn decor in the middle of a nervous breakdown. David held her hand during the prayer, as if they were in love all this time.

"Bless us, O Lord, for these, thy gifts, which we are about to receive, from thy bounty, through Christ our Lord. Amen."

Following the *amen,* I thanked God personally for giving me this thrilling holiday entertainment.

As Eric and I said goodbye to the Fritz family, Janeane pulled me in for a hug.

"Sorry things were a little nuts earlier. Thanksgiving can be hectic," she said.

"I'm sorry I poured you wine. I didn't know—"

"We're all just doing the best we can," she answered.

Janeane was right. Although something as simple as placing food on the table may seem like a small task, a million small tasks add up to a giant undertaking. And that can be a lot to handle, especially on your own. So do the best you can, and if that means taking a sharp blade to a neighbor's lawn decorations, SO BE IT.

Black Friday

The Black Friday holiday peaked around 2008, when the Great Recession forced people to go to stores at 2:00 a.m. the day after Thanksgiving just so they could get a DVD of *The Devil Wears Prada* for two dollars and fight a single mom over a Dyson vacuum that was thirty dollars off. I once saw a sixtysomething Ohio man punch a younger gentleman for a Ryobi drill at Walmart. He cold-cocked his honky ass to save thirteen dollars. It was the best of times, and more than that, it was the worst of times.

Society hasn't fully processed those years in the early aughts when Black Friday kept heightening in absurdity. Year after year, we would turn on the news to find women pummeled to death in the name of an MP3 player doorbuster deal. I wish I could act as though I were above it, but I was right there among the frugal people, running into a Target while it was still dark out, smile on my face. In fact, to be fully transparent, here I am in a local Cleveland paper, seen hauling ass for a nine-dollar copy of *Mario Kart* on Wii...

(That's me in the hat and scarf, perfect running form as I headed inside.)

That day, I saw things no human should ever see, a dark side of retail and consumerism that we must never revisit. It is pertinent that we learn from our mistakes, and I tell this tale not to make you laugh, no, but to caution you to never repeat the evils of the past—specifically Black Friday pre-2010.

It was 2007, and no less than twenty-four hours earlier, I was waking up at my parents' house to watch Nikki Blonsky perform "You Can't Stop the Beat" from *Hairspray* atop an Amica insurance float at the Macy's Thanksgiving Day Parade. I was living on my own for the first time, nary a disposable fund in my bank account. I had maybe sixty dollars to my name, and I needed to buy gifts for parents, siblings, and significant others of siblings, *and* I had a brand-new home to furnish. Times were tough, so I convinced my older brother and Mom to join me for an early morning shopping trip at the nearby Ohio outlet center.

We would hit up Target at 5:00, right when they opened, then head off to the Walmart next door, followed by a stop at Kohl's, which opened an hour later. Mom had her wad of Kohl's cash at the ready like she always does, never not prepared to get a discount on whatever pajamas and word art she decides to buy. After Kohl's, we would head back home for some fuel (left-over stuffing and mashed potatoes covered in day-old gravy) before heading back out to the actual mall, where we would do the specialty shops.

If we wanted to get any deals at Target, we would have to get there early and wait in line. Fortunately, employees were handing out coffee and candy canes before opening the doors, so we had sustenance while we waited alongside other customers. Just a few yards ahead of us in line were people who'd brought sleeping bags and spent the night. When asked what they'd camped out for, they said "a GPS system." We're so lucky that nowadays our phones tell us where to drive, because back then, we had to buy entirely different gadgets in place of paper maps, and if you were strapped for cash, you would have to literally sleep at the store to get one at a reasonable price.

Behind us in line, I met a woman named Thisa, a name

I remembered because she corrected me when I thought her name was Lisa. "No, it's Thisa, like class thesis, but Thisa." Everyone was tired and making little sense, but somehow, I understood exactly what she meant.

Once inside, I ran to the back of the store by the electronics. Mom went to housewares, and my older brother went to tools. Everyone was in a mad scramble to get their discounted wares, including my old friend Thisa, who was in the market for a PlayStation 3. They were an incredibly hot item that year, almost impossible to get. Most places didn't even have a discount on them, but stores were advertising to get people through the doors in hopes they would buy other things while on the hunt. I'm guessing each location got about five consoles, three of which were accounted for by seasonal employees. In the rush to get one of the remaining two, Thisa tossed aside a young girl who got in her way. When I say tossed aside, I mean Thisa threw her like a rag doll. This child must've been about seven years old, and Thisa put her right foot in front of the kid and then used her hand to push her out of the way. I'd never seen anything like it. Under ordinary circumstances, a crowd would've reprimanded this adult for being so physical with a child, but no one has any sense at 5:00 a.m. when they're shopping for a deal and loaded with last night's tryptophan.

Back in electronics, there was a table setup with video game systems. A big sign said SONY and had a wall of PlayStation 2s surrounding a small quantity of the new PlayStation 3s. The employees were obviously trying to trick consumers, who likely assumed the newer system would be either on a table by itself or behind a glass.

I, of course, was just looking to get my copy of *Mario Kart*, which wasn't as tough to grab. I got my game and held it tight, then started looking at the other discounts. If you've ever done Black Friday, you know it's called Black Friday because you simply black out when shopping. The Krampus spirit takes over, and you lose all sense of normalcy, grabbing whatever is in your path. I only budgeted for one Wii game, yet I was grabbing other items that it seemed like the other shoppers wanted. There was an area with one lone waffle maker left, so I grabbed it. Other people were fighting over boxes of Monopoly for a dollar, so I grabbed one of those too. It didn't matter that I already had Monopoly and hadn't played it for over ten years or that I don't make waffles; I was buying these items. Why? Because I grabbed them before other people who also wanted them. Somewhere in the haze, I noticed Thisa out of the corner of my eye.

"Give me the fucking PlayStation!" she shouted at a little old lady.

"It's my fucking PlayStation!" the little old lady shouted back, f-bombs aplenty, as a crowd gathered around the two women as if it were a UFC fight.

While the two sparring partners were playing tug-of-war with the box, the young girl Thisa had tossed aside earlier was circling the grown women. I noticed her getting closer and closer to Thisa.

"Thisa, be careful. There's a child!" I said, warning my

violent line friend about the kid she'd already gone one round with and won.

Thisa ignored me, glaring directly into the eyes of the octogenarian on a quest for a new machine to play *Crash Bandicoot* on.

The little girl crept closer and closer as Thisa dug her heels into the store tile. Before I could warn Thisa again, she backed her ass (literally) up into the child.

This time, the young girl flew across the aisle, screaming. Only it wasn't a normal scream; it was what I can only describe as a Disney Channel scream. If you've ever turned on the Disney Channel only to see a young actor aggressively performing mannerisms and facial tics completely detached from reality, then you know this scream. And that's exactly what this girl did. Like a caffeinated Hannah Montana. And Thisa stopped in her tracks to join in!

"You see what you made me do? That little girl is hurt!" she shouted at the old woman, still clutching the PlayStation 3.

"That's not my fault!" the elderly woman responded.

"Hey! Stop this right now!" an employee shouted, finally getting everyone to settle down as he helped the little girl up. "This is out of hand!"

I noticed the child had a cry face but no tears. Like a Real Housewife on a reunion couch talking to Andy Cohen, she was simply looking for sympathy.

"You okay?" the employee asked her.

"I was just trying to get the PlayStation for my older brother and these two ladies knocked me out."

"Give her the video game!" a woman nearby shouted, encouraging other consumers to join in her chant.

The scene was something out of a movie, with strangers banding together to chastise the two adults fighting over a gaming console until both their hearts grew two sizes and they handed it over to the little kid. The child skipped away with her PlayStation 3 in hand. With the attention span of a dog, the crowd immediately dispersed and went about the rest of their discounting to fight with each other over other goods. A man ripped a *Shrek the Third* plush out of the hands of another adult man. Two twentysomething women fought over a one-dollar bath bomb. Chaos. It's hard to describe war to people who haven't found themselves in the middle of the fight, but trust and believe that there were casualties that morning, all before sunrise.

After paying for my Wii game, the waffle maker and Monopoly board, a copy of the second Twilight book (which I still haven't read), and strawberry-chocolate lip gloss in a container that looked like a purse, which I told everyone was for my cousin Natalie but was really for myself, I met my brother and Mom to check out their hauls. They had tools for my dad, a sweater for my brother, and various holiday decorations for my parents' house—the standard fare, which we loaded into the trunk of my mom's SUV. Mom used a cart, which she asked me to return to the cart rack, so like any other asshole, I simply wheeled the cart to the nearest place where no one would see me abandon it. That place was an empty parking spot, which happened to be next to a brand-new Lexus. Inside, it was loaded with finds from Black Friday shopping.

Just as I was walking away from our discarded cart, I heard the beeping of the doors unlocking and a familiar voice...

"Throw these bags in the back really quick—"

It was Thisa! I was ready to offer my condolences for her not getting the PlayStation 3 she had been fighting for earlier. But before I could get out the words, I saw the young girl she'd tossed like a football, now holding the PlayStation 3.

"Thanks, Mom. Go ahead to Kohl's, and I'll be right behind you."

"Sara! What did I tell you?" Thisa scolded.

"Oh, right, sorry. I won't call you *Mom* again," Sara replied.

Thisa and Sara were holiday scammers! Have you ever seen the movie *Heartbreakers* with Sigourney Weaver and Jennifer Love Hewitt? They were like that, only instead of using cleavage to con men, they were weaponizing holiday cheer to scam Sony PlayStations from a Midwest shopping center.

What I couldn't figure out was why Thisa had pushed her daughter upon entering the store. My theory is that they intended to fight each other over the PlayStation, hoping the crowd would remember how mean the adult was to the child and encourage her to turn it over, thereby ensuring no one else got the machine. Instead, a third party was involved. I pose this question to you—was the initial store push part of their cahoots?

I didn't tell anyone that day what I witnessed, worried we had all already seen so much darkness, what with soccer moms shoving people out of the way for eight-dollar three-wicks. I can't even remember the last time someone was trampled to death for a DVD player. Those of us on the front lines during those 2000s and 2010s Black Fridays will never forget some images we saw in the wee hours of the morning. We will be forever haunted by the screams and violence we clocked some of our contemporaries displaying on a quest for doorbusters. Only now can we begin to heal, looking back at the faults of yesteryear to ensure we don't repeat the mistakes of yore. Black Friday is now known as a relatively calm shopping day, but real ones know that those two words stand for all the fallen soldiers who never made it to see how far we've come. May we always remember those items we lost and the lives we compromised in the name of discounted Panasonic TVs that came with a free ten-dollar gift card for your next purchase before the following Tuesday.

Holiday Tip

Be careful what you wear to group functions. Below is a picture of a sweater I wore on Thanksgiving. It was one of the years I *did* make it back to Ohio. After dinner with my family, I made the rounds in my hometown, visiting friends from high school. Upon my arrival for dessert at one of my old besties', her elderly grandma saw me from across the room and sent a potent stink eye my way. Turns out her vision was fading, so when she squinted to see me at the other end of the table, she thought I showed up at the Midwest home in a crop top. While there's nothing wrong with a man in a crop top, I wouldn't bare midriff in the cold Ohio month of November.

Upon further reflection, it *does* appear as though I was showing off my stomach. Oops.

The lesson here is that you should always photograph yourself in various lights and angles before leaving the house in your new festive sweater.

(They tell me this photo will appear in black and white, but just know that in full Technicolor, the bottom half looks like the same tone as my skin.)

Birds Actually

Birds are not for me. They're so unpredictable, they poop everywhere, and I find them terrifying. Alfred Hitchcock knew this, and so should you all. I've always felt a bit haunted by birds, and it's not just me. My mom, Linda, has also been plagued by the winged creatures for many years, more recently by a bold-ass woodpecker I discussed in my first book. But that woodpecker wasn't the only bold fowl that gave me and my mom a hard time. Years earlier, another bird nested in a fall wreath Mom made for our front door.

I live for autumnal decorations. Give me pumpkins and gourds and spooky skeletons to scatter around the house, and I'm happy as a clam. I can tablescape the shit out of the dining room with a quick trip to HomeGoods. My dream is to one day have the wealth and space necessary to sub out all my regular dinnerware and glassware for their seasonal counterparts, things shaped like pumpkins and printed with leaves. But when it comes to outdoor decor, I'm wary, and much like Meryl Streep in *Doubt*, I have doubts.

Mom used to collect foliage, things like pine cones and leaves, and always found creative ways to use them throughout our house. We would gather pretty leaves and press them into a cute picture, and every year, she would head on over to Joann Fabric for a wreath base to fill with her outdoor finds. But that all stopped when a bird nested in her homemade statement piece.

My brothers had already moved off to college, and I was the only kid living at the family home. I got back from high school one day and did what I always did: watched *TRL* while snacking. Around 5:30, Mom got home from work and started to make a pasta dinner. Dad was working late, and leaving water boiling, Mom went to the front door to get a package that was delivered, and one of the nesting creatures flew right into our home.

"Dan! Help! A bird is in the house!" Mom screamed at the top of her lungs.

I came running to find my mom, disheveled and fearful, a state I wish I could say made me want to help, but instead it made me laugh instantly (teenagers are rude!). My demeanor quickly changed when the pigeon flew past me and into the spare bedroom that had previously belonged to my older brother.

"Turn off the stove and bring me the pot with the lid," Mom instructed. All mothers have a switch they can flip; it happens very quickly, and we all know the one. They can be fragile and scared one minute, but as soon as they decide to take care of business, look out. Linda P. flipped the switch, and that bird was screwed.

I handed her the pot and lid, and she stormed into the spare room before closing the door behind her. It was just her and the fowl. From the outside, it sounded like a brawl. There were all sorts of sounds: wood furniture banging against the drywall, wings frantically flapping in the air, jolts and bumps and screams that could've been coming from either the bird or Mom. Unclear. What *was* clear was when Mom opened the door, victorious. She carefully held the lid on the pot and made her way past me in the hallway.

"Call Pizza Hut, Danster. I'm not cookin' anymore tonight."

She had had enough. But before she could get to the door to release the wild animal, my dad entered from a long day of work.

"Hi, hon," he said to my mom, who looked like she'd just gotten into a fight with a lawn mower. "You cooking?"

"There's a bird in here, Gar."

"Nice! Chicken?" he asked, naively hoping she was making one of his favorite dishes.

"IT'S A LIVE BIRD, GARY!" she replied.

"Well, are you gonna cook it?"

Dad should've just kept quiet and enjoyed the pizza when it arrived because Mom was in no mood to placate him. She made her way to the front door, lifted the lid off the pot, and let the bird fly back out into the wild. With her feathered friend in the rearview, she slammed the door shut behind her and handed my dad her cookware.

"Clean this pot and take the wreath off the door. I'm taking a bath," she said. "By the way, there's bird shit on the steps. Can you wipe it up, Gar? I need some me time."

"Why the hell are you bringing birds in the house?" Dad asked as she made her way upstairs.

"You think I mailed the bird an invite, Gar? It nested in the wreath!"

"You're mailin' a million holiday cards this time of year, so who knows what else you give to the postman..." Dad joked under his breath.

"You better fly away from me with that attitude, Gary. Now give your son money for the pizza guy."

I told Dad the details of what had happened while we waited for the grub, and he was impressed by how his wife had handled it. Men of his generation liked to act tough, to be in charge, but they knew their wives were the ones handling it all. He witnessed his be a superhero by giving birth to three boys, and now he knew she could handle whatever wild animals might fly her way. Nothing stands a chance when it gets in the way of a mom.

I've learned the holidays are all about birds. Halloween is filled with winged imagery: crows are everywhere at

HomeGoods, Harry Potter has his owl, and the aforementioned Hitchcock movie is a television staple in October. November is all about cooking (and then eating) a bird, before moving into December when carolers sing "Twelve Days of Christmas," a song that is all about, you guessed it, *birds*. In fact, days one through four and six through seven are all bird related. Hugh Grant said in *Love Actually* that love is all around, but I've got my own sneaky feeling that you'll find birds actually are all around.

End of the World

It was October. We met under the bleachers as football fans from our little town were seated above. Your T-shirt advertised the high school team, even though we wouldn't be ninth graders for another three years. You liked my friend, but he wandered off with your friend, so it was just the two of us. The aluminum stands started shaking as people stomped along with a cheer led by the pom-pom-holding popular girls we would come to envy.

"The world is ending. Come quick! The sky is falling. Follow me!" you lied, grabbing my hand and leading me to a quaint dark section underneath the cheering townspeople. You were playing pretend, and I forever longed for an escape from my reality. We were a perfect match.

—

In twelfth grade, I grabbed your shaky hand backstage at the talent show. I eased your fears about performing in front of our classmates. I wasn't scared because you were next to me. We named our characters Pancake and Syrup, which was so corny, but it made us laugh for years to come. Ever since then, I could remind you of Pancake and Syrup, and we'd be right back in that moment, an inside joke that would last a lifetime.

"I'm sad we won't get to see each other next year when we're at college," you said.

"I'll visit all the time," I lied as I led you onstage into the light.

—

At twenty-two, I called you on the phone from my new city. My heart was racing, and I was afraid to say the words out loud. You could hear the fear in my voice and quickly took hold of the conversation until I was at a calm 59 BPM.

"I'm gay."

"I love you," you replied.

—

We lived in the same city again a few years later. Our first New Year's Eve was planned—a dinner party and a couple of bar stops. I wanted to run into my crush, so we headed his way. You poured us too many cocktails, and my rude side came out.

"Go home and get some sleep," I said as I closed the cab door and directed the driver to your apartment. If I'd had two fewer cocktails, I would've ridden passenger to ensure you stumbled home okay. Cocktails sometimes got in our way.

—

You knocked on my door in the spring, with swollen eyes after a fight with a boyfriend. We sat on my bed and talked through each detail. By midnight, we were laughing about nonsense and planning our elaborate futures. We promised to let men come and go, and you assured me that we would be on our rocking chairs at the end, laughing about our nonsense.

—

Our first vacation together was my favorite. Another October. Twentysomething bliss. Our eyes filled with happy tears as we laughed uncontrollably and sang old Cher songs at the top of our lungs for three days straight. We had great travel chemistry and always loosened up when we were far from our responsibilities. Getting away was good for us. We needed to reconnect. I told you about a new guy I was dating, and we stayed up late trying to decide whether he was worth it. You were single, so you encouraged me to kick him to the curb. I did. He was collateral damage.

—

Not quite thirty, we were packing a truck with the things you'd collected over the years. You were headed back to the city with the bleachers, and I was moving in with my new, other, other half. Things hadn't been the same for a while. I went down one road, you took another, and each passing moment, we lost a bit of what made us special. If the love we started with weren't enough to last a hundred lifetimes, we would've become strangers.

—

You visited for a weekend shortly thereafter, one foot in your new life, the other firmly planted in the one we had together. My depression was strong, but through the fog, I saw your face, and it grounded me. You were the only one I told because you felt safe. I wished you didn't have to leave.

—

Our bimonthly calls became painfully routine during our early thirties, and no longer being tied together by geography was a challenge for us. I asked about your dates, and you politely championed my career achievements the way a new friend thinks they're supposed to. Those elaborate futures we'd imagined years ago looked nothing like what we'd built.

—

You had an issue with your folks in 2019. Although you had a new boyfriend whom you loved, he didn't know them yet the way I did, so you called me.

"I don't know what to do," you cried.

"I love you," I replied.

—

Just shy of thirty-three, you rang to tell me you were engaged to the man of your dreams. The two of you were heading to yet another city for a fresh start. Despite the physical and emotional distance, you asked me to be by your side when you told him you do.

"I wouldn't miss you walking down the aisle," I lied unknowingly.

—

The world changed six months later. You called me from a car in your white dress, minutes before you would have a new ring on your finger. It took a pandemic to make me miss your wedding day, but I knew you were in good hands with your eventual husband. He would hold you as your heart soared.

—

November 2020. Things kept getting worse, and it had me thinking about you. I drank straight from a bottle of merlot, listening to that old Cher song we liked, and I remembered the nights we had too much together. I missed your rude side. I was feeling too emo to call, but I chased a shot of vino with a text to your phone. It was an old photo of us at a bar, young and happy. You hearted it.

Someone who lived in my building passed away that day. I didn't know him, but someone did. Someone calmed him when his heart raced, and now his other other would be without him. The news said things were worse than we thought. Everyone walked around in masks, but at least our eyes were free, right? Maybe it would be better if the masks covered our eyes so we wouldn't have to see the tragedy around us.

—

Christmas is extra tough. I hope Judy is right that someday soon we all will be together. I'm sentimental for holidays past, when we were in the same town, and you would come over and see my parents. You would hug my brothers and kneel to say hello to my young nieces. You fit in with my family because you are my family. I daydream about a normal Christmas, surrounded by the smiles of everyone I love. I'm nostalgic for moments that I'm not even sure will ever happen again.

The sky feels like it's falling again. The bleachers are shaking, and I know one of your hands is tied up with holding your husband's hand, your daughter's hand, your parents' hands, your siblings, your other friends, but could I have the other? Could I follow you into the darkness one more time? I'll bring along the people I'm holding with my other hand, and we can all muddle through together. Is there enough room under the bleachers? It's been a couple of years since I've seen you in person, but none of that matters right now. Even if your mask is on, I'll remember your eyes. I'd recognize them filled with tears, love, disgust, or fear, and you would recognize mine—they haven't changed too much. Not many people have seen every look in my eyes, but we have the nights and years on our side. We have the *I love yous* and the inside jokes and the phone calls. We have Pancake and Syrup. If the sky falls, it would be okay because we were lucky to have enough friendship to last a lifetime, filled with the good and the bad. Maybe the sky needs to fall to bring us together again.

My Favorite Things

Buying the perfect gift for someone is a special skill. I used to think I had the talent, but I find that every year around Christmas, I get overwhelmed by the list of people I need to buy for, and I give up. That's when I log online and order ten of whatever gift set Oprah is shilling on her favorite things list. My nearest and dearest have gotten more truffle salt than they know what to do with. When my brother kindly informed me that he's still polishing off the fancy sodium I gave him the year prior, I forced him to watch *Hocus Pocus* and reminded him that salt wards off evil spirits. My gift was a service, and I encouraged him to use it to fight sassy witch trios in the event any virgins in town light a black-flame candle! I like to think I'm easy to shop for—I enjoy video games and pop culture junk I don't need. Get me a Rosie O'Donnell Barbie or something Nintendo, and I'm good as gold. Really anything nostalgic will bring a smile to my face, which brings me to holiday 2019.

Over Thanksgiving weekend, my boyfriend and I decided

to binge old episodes of MTV's *Newlyweds* featuring Jessica Simpson and Nick Lachey. It wasn't widely available to stream, but we found a bootleg version online that had each episode broken into thirty-minute chunks. In one of the episodes from the early 2000s, Jessica is seen doing a photo shoot for a dessert beauty line that was advertised as "lickable." The products were incredibly popular when I was in high school, but unfortunately, I was so closeted that I was afraid to purchase them for myself. I got a lotion for a friend as a birthday gift junior year, hoping she would leave it in my car one night, but alas, it never happened.

Upon rewatch, I mentioned to my boyfriend just how badly I had wanted the product during my youth.

"I'm so jealous of teenagers now who are so comfortable with their sexuality. I was always so afraid to like the things I liked. I worried people would judge me," I told him.

"You wanted lickable body products when you were sixteen?" he asked.

"I *needed* lickable body products when I was sixteen. It seemed so aspirational to me. I fantasized about having a boyfriend who wouldn't be able to resist licking me once I applied her products," I explained.

In the *Newlyweds* episode, Jessica is doing the promotional ads for her line and ends up with an upset stomach from the shoot. A red flag if there ever was one. Yet still, I wanted nothing more than the banana split body frosting and the cotton candy sugar-shimmer body powder of my own.

There's *a lot* I know about Jessica Simpson. In my first book, there's an entire chapter dedicated to my queen. But of course, there are some facts I'm fuzzy on. For instance, I *know* she has a successful fashion brand, but I don't know much more than what I've seen on the shopping channels when I watch her hawk her anaconda pant or kitten-heeled shoes. I naively assumed the lickable body products were still in production in 2019. After all, it was something everyone wanted in 2004, so I assumed it was a thriving part of her brand.

My boyfriend is one of those excellent gift givers I mentioned earlier. He surprises me with thoughtful birthday gifts and romantic Valentine's Day presents, and he always remembers our anniversaries. We started dating around the time of the first iPad, and I'll never forget when he re-created *that* scene from *Love Actually*. You know, the one where Andrew Lincoln shows up at Keira Knightley's house with giant cue cards to confess his love for her, even though she *just* married his bestie? But instead of cue cards, my boyfriend used his new iPad and filmed himself scrolling slides with romantic messages on each one. (I hadn't gotten hitched to his best friend, so it was a less inappropriate and more sincere version than what ultimately appeared in the film.)

He's also great about getting me those nostalgic gifts from my childhood, taking notes throughout the year and then perusing eBay. One year, he got me a collection of Nickelodeon magazines. Another time, he gave me HitClips—remember those small square gadgets that played less than a minute of a song?

The quality was bad, and you never got to hear the bridge, but they were cute nonetheless. Then, on Christmas 2019, I opened a misshapen package wrapped in Frosty the Snowman paper, only to discover my very own gift set of Jessica Simpson lickable body products! I was thrilled!

In retrospect, perhaps I should've known that the product was one of his online-auction finds instead of a current line of goods, but…that's not what happened. I set the treats aside and opened a few other gifts, grateful to have such a thoughtful significant other. Still, when friends and family asked what he gave me for Christmas, I mentioned everything *but* the Jessica Simpson stuff. Even though I was an out gay man, I had some residual shame left over from my teen years. Telling people I received bath and body products targeted to women was not something I was strong enough to do in 2019.

Days went by, and the potions sat on my bathroom counter, unopened. With Christmas break wrapping up and just a few more days left before going back to work, we decided to smoke a little weed we found in an old drawer. Marijuana is not something I partake in often because I have zero self-control when it comes to eating. In fact, knowing that I was going to smoke, I decided to get rid of all the holiday treats we had been indulging in throughout December. Diet was starting. Unfortunately, the weed had other plans and jump-started my typical cravings.

"I'm starving!" I told my boyfriend.

"There's some pretzel slims and almonds in the cupboard," he informed.

I've never been someone who can survive off pretzel slims and almonds. Pretzels are already slim enough—why did someone decide to make them thinner? And nothing infuriates me more than when I open a magazine or turn on a talk show and see a nutritionist instructing people to eat a handful of almonds as a snack. First of all, they don't actually mean a handful; they mean four individual almonds. That's not a handful. Second, that's not enough. I'm six three and have a healthy sweet tooth. Give me a king-size Kit Kat and at least two sleeves of Oreos or nothing at all.

"I'm gonna order food," I said.

"No ordering food! We promised we would start eating healthy and saving money," he reminded me.

Fuck. I hate when he's right. And I was hungry! I excused myself to our apartment restroom so I could devise a plan to get food. I quietly raided the drawers next to the toilet in my high state. I found a few Luden's cough drops, which are basically Life Savers candy, and since they are technically medicine, it means they don't have to put nutrition facts on the packaging, which I take to mean that I can eat as many as I want, and it doesn't count toward any calorie counts. Out of the corner of my eye, I spotted something else edible: the Jessica Simpson lickable lotion.

You can all imagine what happened next. I know you're disgusted, but I was high and decided to eat it! Stop judging me! People eat crazy shit when they're stoned! My old college roommate once put a Kool-Aid packet in bong water because he was thirsty. This was lickable, so it was basically like whipped cream! Besides, I wasn't spooning it out of the bottle—I was simply putting a bit on my arm and licking it off. At least that's how it started. The first bite was what I would call "dainty," but the weed was strong, and suddenly I was like a Hoover vacuum, sucking it up and chasing it with cherry cough drops. My boyfriend eventually knocked on the door, wondering where I had been for so long. Time has a way of stopping when you're high, so I honestly don't know how long I was in there eating old moisturizer with a side of cough medicine, but it was long enough that it was a cause of concern for him.

"Be right out!" I said.

Exiting the bathroom, I felt satisfied and no longer craved sugar. We sat down to watch *The Family Stone*, and by the end, I was no longer stoned. I started the film like Luke Wilson when he's high and finds out Diane Keaton's character is going to pass away, and I ended the film as sober as SJP when the movie starts. Does that make sense? Although I was no longer high by the end of the night, my stomach started to turn.

Around midnight, we headed to the bedroom to get some sleep, but as soon as the lights went out, my insides felt like they were on a roller coaster. My boyfriend drifted off to dreamland while I sat on the cold tile of the bathroom floor. I've never felt such pain in my life. I always thought I had a tough stomach. Sure, I've gotten the occasional food poisoning from gas station sushi or a cheap vacation buffet, but never had I felt so bad. And it just kept getting worse. Aside from a dry heave, nothing was coming out of me. Maybe the cough drops blocked the outlets. As I hunched over, holding my tummy and praying for relief, I looked up at the counter and noticed the beauty product I had stuffed my face with. I gathered my strength and reached for the butterscotch-toffee shimmer mist. I turned the bottle and noticed a manufacture date. It was 2006. Thirteen years prior. Oops.

I survived most of the night, but by sunrise, I knew I had to go to the emergency room.

"Boo, can you take me to the ER? My stomach isn't right," I said as I shook my partner awake.

"Must've been something you ate, but didn't we have the same food yesterday?" he asked.

"Well...look, I just need to get to a doctor," I countered.

The way to the hospital was rough. My stomach cramps were not letting up, and I didn't know what to do. When we arrived, the clumsy holiday crowd filled the emergency room. I signed in at the front desk but knew I couldn't wait my turn. There was an alien inside me trying to get out.

A nurse saw my coloring was bad and sat me in a wheelchair and drove me to see the nearest doctor.

"What did you eat?" the nurse asked.

"Um...I mean, it's the holiday season. What didn't I eat?" At least I didn't lie.

I did everything I could to buy myself time. Moans and screams came out of me, but some of them were just a way for me to stall as I figured out how to explain that I ate something that (probably) wasn't even fully FDA approved back in 2006 when it was manufactured. Before I could answer, a specialist entered the room.

"Sounds like you have appendicitis," he said with confidence. "We'll run some tests, and you might need to have an emergency appendectomy."

He seemed so sure of himself. So sure, in fact, that I wasn't interested in telling anyone around what happened that night before. Until now in this book. I had my appendix removed, and post-surgery, I suffered from some internal digestive issues that lasted months and months. I saw stomach specialists and internal medicine experts, all of whom were unsure how to diagnose me. Each of them asked what my diet was like, but none of them knew I ate something a pop star advertised over a decade earlier.

My stomach is good now, as I believe the affliction has finally passed. There's no real way to know exactly what happened to me, but for years, I have dealt with the guilt of not telling any of the professionals I saw that I accidentally got high and ate a bunch of stuff that wasn't meant to be consumed since Bush was in office. Even then, it was only meant to be licked. LICKED! A way to spice up sexy time with your hunky boy-bander boyfriend, not a meal replacement. Hunger got the best of me, and I inhaled a pop-star-endorsed lotion that wasn't meant to replace cupcakes. The good news is that I survived and no longer have to worry about my appendix bursting at an inopportune time. Now that I no longer hold my secret, I can release the shame I felt for so many years. It remains to this day my sweetest sin.

Black Velvet

Mrs. Claus does not get enough respect for my liking. In the nonreligious lore of Christmas, Santa is the one people often dress up as, the one who does all the work delivering presents, the guy children sit on at the mall to take pictures with, and even the one who gets movies made about his life. Tim Allen, Ed Asner, Kurt Russell, Alec Baldwin, Jim Broadbent, Bryan Cranston, and James Earl Jones have all portrayed the red-suited heifer in live-action or animated films. The list for Mrs. Claus is much shorter, and they often have much less to do.

The micro issue is that media portrays Mrs. Claus as some little old biddy who occasionally gives Saint Nick a pep talk before he goes off on some big adventure. The macro is that women are never treated fairly, even in Christmas fables. Where's Mrs. Claus's big adventure?

I've decided that since history has not given Mrs. Claus a big adventure on Christmas, I'm going to do it myself. So sit tight, little bear, because I'm about to tell you the story of

Mrs. Carole Marie DeBella-Claus and the holiday she finally snapped.

'Twas the night before Christmas, when all through the house, Mrs. Claus was preparing to help her hubby out...

"Hon, I know you have a long night ahead of you, but could you please pick up after yourself? You barely watched half an episode of *Shark Tank* tonight, and there are cookie crumbs all over the couch. I'm not your mother," Carole gently says to her husband, Nick, a.k.a. Santa, as she vacuums the cushions for the third time that week.

It's Christmas Eve, and they've danced this dance before. Carole spends the day making sure everything is perfect for her other half. She presses his clothes, makes him dinner, and even carefully irons his red velvet hat so it lies properly on his head when he's going in and out of chimneys. It's the biggest night of Nick's career, and Carole supervises, making sure the i's are dotted and the t's are crossed. Year after year since they were married, Nick rides off in his sleigh at sundown, not to return until sunrise. He says it takes that long to deliver all the presents to the kids, but Carole has her doubts. She wonders how it could take *exactly* that amount of time every year, even as the world population grows and technology advances. It wasn't until recently that Carole's mind started to wonder about her husband's yearly whereabouts. But after decades of marriage, she doesn't have the strength to care if he's dropping bikes under the trees of good children or spending the late hours in a dimly lit massage parlor with a sex worker named Dina getting his rocks off. *Better her than me,* Carole says to herself.

"Did you—"

"Give Rudolph his meds, yes," Carole replies. Rudolph is great at his job, but only because Carole sneaks half a Benadryl into his carrot before the night begins. Otherwise, his manic energy would make the flight shakier than a helicopter.

"Speaking of pills, did you take your decongestant?" Carole asks, knowing Nick needs it for the night ahead in so many different environments. She's had to start putting it out for him since the one year he went into the medicine cabinet himself. The sinus pill is blue just like Nick's Viagra. He accidentally took the wrong one in '09 and had trouble fitting down the chimneys. He came home with a nose redder than Rudolph's from all the extra snot, and the once-tight elastic band around his pants fit more like a suggestion.

"Yes, I already took my Mucinex. I'm going to—"

"Go ahead and shower. I'll print out your checklist."

Carole was always finishing her husband's sentences, but the problem was, he never finished hers. They went through the motions of a happy marriage, but she has wanted more for a *very* long time, and it all came to a head each year when she was left alone with her thoughts while Nick traveled the world solo. Carole wondered if there was anything else out there for her, another man to fulfill her needs. She was tired of being left alone on everyone else's happiest night.

Carole would usually drink herself into *It's a Wonderful Life* mode and think about what could have been with former flames. It wasn't like Nick was the only man she ever had. A few years back, she'd strayed when her husband left for work and Carole invited Jack Frost over. After a couple of peppermint shots, she thought she and Jack could run away together, start a new life, but his body wasn't the only thing that was cold that night. After they hooked up, Jack told her he wasn't interested in a relationship, and Carole had gone back to her routine life with Nick. Men were always taking what they wanted from Carole and leaving her to pick up the pieces. Still, she considered what her routine could have been with Jack or one of the other men who let her down before she settled with Nick in her early twenties.

Carole laid Nick's seasonal costume on the bed: the red velvet jacket, black leather belt, Kmart boots, and a candy cane treat for a midnight energy boost in between cookies and milk. As she set the peppermint candy on the white undershirt, she heard the pitter-patter of reindeer on the roof. Dasher, Dancer, Prancer, Vixen, Comet, Cupid, Donner, Blitzen, and a fully Zen Rudolph were all ready to fly Santa around the world, all while Carole put on her face mask, poured a glass of bed wine, and caught up on *The Real Housewives of Beverly Hills*.

"Carole, are we out of the Philosophy gingerbread body wash?" Nick asked from the nearby shower.

Carole had tried to order more of his favorite shower gel earlier that week, but the company was sold out of their limited-edition inventory. "They were out. I called to see if Sephora had any—"

"Did you tell them who I am?"

"No, I didn't tell them who you are, Nick. I—"

As the words left her bright red lip, she caught a glimpse of herself in the fogged-up mirror. Realizing she was no longer the young girl who was so impressed by a jolly man who works one day a year, she wanted to tell everyone who the hell *she* is, not who her husband is. And she didn't just want to tell the woman working the holiday phone lines at Sephora but the man she married who was bare-ass naked in the shower while Carole organized his entire life. He would crumble without her, and he didn't seem to care about her life in the slightest.

Perfect certainly wasn't the adjective to describe Carole either, because even she knew she had her own set of hang-ups. No one reaches the finish line of life as a total angel. She reveled in gossip, always sided with the villains on her favorite reality TV shows, and often found herself chasing a nonprescribed Vicodin with budget tequila when she really needed five hundred milligrams of ibuprofen and a nap.

"Carole, I work one night a year. All I ask is that you have the body wash I like for this one night!" Nick shouted at her as if she were his child.

"All you ask? ALL YOU ASK? I DO EVERYTHING FOR YOU, NICHOLAS! EVERYTHING! Ya know what? That's it. I've had it. I'm taking the sleigh," she said as she walked out of the house grabbing a bottle of wine, draped a winter coat over her arm, and slammed the front door behind her. Carole had finally had enough.

“What? Carole?” Nick screamed from the shower, unclear what was happening outside the steady rainfall and unable to see through the soapy water in his eyes from a body wash that didn’t hit the same as Philosophy’s seasonal scents.

Outside their quaint home was a ladder leading up to the roof. A ladder that her husband worshipped. Sometimes Carole felt like Nick would rather be at Home Depot or out in the yard with his ladder than inside with her. She hated that ladder and everything it represented. After using it to climb on the roof to the sleigh, Carole pulled it up behind her so Nick couldn’t follow her *or* spend the evening with his precious purchase.

“Carole, where are you going? Put the ladder down so I can come up there,” Nick said as he ran out of the house in a towel that could barely wrap around his belly full of cookies.

“No, I’ll be back in the morning.”

Carole hopped into the sleigh and said a decisive, "Go." *Go* was all the animals needed to make magic happen, to lift the sleigh off the roof tiles that Nick had forgotten to replace earlier that year. Carole always hated when her husband would do a reindeer roll call to get them moving, knowing it was all pomp and circumstance. The creatures didn't need to hear him say, "On Dasher, on Dancer, on Prancer, and Vixen" etc. It was so patronizing to the deer. No shit they had to fly; they did the same trip every single year. Nick just liked the attention of it all and the power it represented.

The reindeer ran for Carole, with air from their hooves causing a windstorm below, blowing Nick's towel off his still-wet body as the sleigh flew through the cold winter air and out of the North Pole. Carole looked down at her naked husband, never more certain that she was making the right decision. Maybe she would've felt differently in the moment and wanted to stay if he had accidentally taken the Viagra earlier.

"What about all the kids' presents?" Nick shouted as she began her ascent.

"I'm getting a present this year! A big one!" Carole replied, smiling as she caught the sad image of her husband's limp junk in the rearview sleigh mirror.

She was on her way, but where to? She didn't know and she didn't care, so long as she got to get away from her house, her life, and her feelings for at least one night. For a split second, she felt a tinge of guilt—guilt that the sack of presents she was traveling with wouldn't get delivered—but then she thought of how all those young kids would learn a lesson in the morning. They would learn that life doesn't always work out the way you think it's going to, and that was a present in itself. Carole reached back and opened one of the gifts meant for a child. It was a karaoke microphone, bedazzled and fully loaded with a catalog of songs to sing along to. On it, she found a familiar jam by Ms. Shania Twain. As the beat kicked in, Carole sang along...

"Let's go, girls!" And with that, Carole was ready to take on the night. The words left her lips and encouraged her first stop—picking up *her* girls, and by girls, I mean her bestie, Sue, and her gay friend, Joel. Into the microphone, she shouted to her caribou drivers, "Stop on Liberty Road!"

The deer rerouted to the address, Joel's house in Arizona, the state where they'd all grown up. Carole knew Sue was already there with Joel because the two spent every Christmas Eve together watching Hallmark's Countdown to Christmas and feeling sorry for themselves.

Joel and Sue were already in their pajamas, one bottle deep into their second Lacey Chabert feature. They were filled with charcuterie and regret—regret that they didn't have the families they'd always imagined they would. What Joel and Sue lacked in kids and grandkids, they made up for in their friendship and love for each other. The two were thick as thieves, and their Christmas wish every year was that they could hang out with the person who completed their triumvirate...Carole. She often missed out on their hangs, excusing herself to be with the elves and wait on her longtime husband to get home from delivering toys.

Despite the usual distance between them all, the three friends were family. Sue would bail Joel out of jail in a minute, and Carole would help the others hide a body if it came to it. It was the kind of unbreakable bond that time, space, and crusty old husbands could never alter.

Joel muted the TV when he heard footsteps above, confident that he wouldn't miss any important plot points without Lacey's familiar dialogue in his ear.

"Girl, do you hear something?" Joel said to Sue as he poured them both another glass of pinot grigio.

"It sounds like...reindeer?"

"Joel and Sue, please come outside immediately!" Carole said, amplified by her bedazzled toy.

"It sounds like—"

"Carole!" they both exclaimed as they popped their heads out of the living room window. Sue and Joel grabbed their coats and full glasses of wine, then ran outside to see Carole and nine reindeer on the roof.

"Carole, what are you doing here?" Sue asked.

"Get in the sleigh. We're going out!" Carole instructed.

Joel was never one to ask questions; he was always ready for a good time. There's someone like him in every friend group. Carole was the responsible one, Sue was the fun one, and Joel was the one who would somehow end up doing lines with an Olsen on a Tuesday night to prove he was spiritually younger than his besties.

Unfortunately, they didn't have a ladder, so Carole had to

make an emergency landing in Sue's backyard with the sleigh. Luckily there was plenty of space, but Prancer did eat all the tomato plants Sue had hoped to regrow in the spring.

"Where we going?" Sue asked.

It was almost midnight on Christmas Eve, so they couldn't do a painting class or goat yoga or ax throwing. Really the only options at 11:59 p.m. on December 24 are church or a bar, and although both places served the kind of red wine Carole liked, only one had a dance floor.

"How about we go for a drink?" Carole suggested.

"How fast are these reindeer?" Joel asked.

"Way faster than your Prius," she countered.

"Rudolph, take us to Clairemont!" Joel shouted as he stepped into the sleigh.

Clairemont is a college town, and specifically, it's *their* college town. Carole, Sue, and Joel had gone to school there, many, many moons ago. They even lived in the same dorm, although Joel was forced to live down the hall since they hadn't allowed boys and girls to share back then.

The campus was mostly empty for winter break, with students home visiting their families. The bars, however, were open for business for locals and stragglers. The three friends parked the sleigh behind a dumpster and metaphorically traveled back in time as they entered a familiar watering hole. They were no longer adults with mortgages and back problems; they were now twenty-year-olds with the world ahead of them and cheap booze available for the drinking.

First stop was a bar called the Junction. It was the place where Sue worked off her loan debt, the place with the bartender who gave Joel his first male-on-male hand job, and the establishment where Carole got engaged to her college sweetheart a week before graduation. It was their Cheers or Central Perk.

"Three Junction Punches!" Joel shouted.

"Are you sure? They're really strong," the local bartender told them.

"Sweetie, we've been drinking Junction Punches since before you were born," Carole said.

"You...you look familiar. Have we...?"

"I'm Carole. Carole Claus. You probably know my husband."

"Oh, you're married."

Maybe I'm single for the night, she thought. After all, she had a whole year to be nice, so she might as well be a little naughty before the clock reset.

As Carole sauntered over to the old jukebox, cocktail in hand, she contemplated what song to play. She scrolled through the selections and saw a number called "Black Velvet" by Alannah Myles, a song that was allegedly about Elvis but sounded like it was written by a glass of whiskey in heat. It was a sexy late-'80's ballad that reminded Carole of her youth. Spring of '89 to be exact. Joel and Sue had taken her to Myrtle Beach for a bachelorette weekend before she tied the knot with Nick. Carole had reservations, but after a few nights partying with friends, she was ready to settle down. That was when her up-and-down feelings about Santa started. One day, she loved him more than anything, and the next, she was contemplating divorce. This was the roller coaster Carole had been on for decades.

Carole put money in the machine and played the song. The sensual guitar strings came over the loudspeaker, and she felt like she was twenty-two again, moving a touch slower than before but keeping up with the beat nonetheless.

A thirty-six-year-old mustached local sat in the corner with a bottle of Blue Moon and took a drag off his cigarette as Carole danced. She called him over to join her. He was a construction worker, a thick-skinned bricklayer named Brick with dry hands and a stretched-out Tweety Bird tattoo along his forearm. Brick hadn't seen Carole and company there before, but he was happy to have people other than college students to look at for a change. Brick longed for the sensual touch of a mature woman after so many nights with drunk sorority girls, immediately fantasizing about what it would be like to kiss a dame like Carole.

"Can I buy you a drink?" he asked.

"I already have one. But you can give me a cigarette," Carole replied, noticing Brick had a pack of Marlboros in his chest pocket.

Brick took out a cig with his rough hands and gently placed it into Carole's mouth, then carefully lit the smoke as Carole kept beat with the song. Feeling his ashy grippers on her lips made Carole long for a man who was different from her husband. A guy who worked with his hands instead of relying on elves to build everything was such a turn-on to her, and the music certainly encouraged her impulses.

"Nothing sexier than black velvet," Brick said as he took a healthy sip of his beer and Alannah Myles sang the sultry chorus.

"Beats red velvet," Carole said as she took a drag, disgusted by the mere thought of her husband back home wearing his Santa costume.

As the second chorus kicked in, Carole began dancing up against Brick, her hips guiding his, her hands reading his thighs like braille. Just as she wondered if Brick had a cell phone in his pocket or something else, she noticed that a young man and woman at a nearby table shot them a look of disgust. Carole didn't care. Society would like Carole to be at home, fixing supper, and making the bed instead of having sex on top of it, and she was tired of it like all women are. Tired of the expectation to lose all sexuality the moment they blow out the candles on their fortieth birthday cake. Tired of trying to live in a society where men get hotter as they age and women become invisible. She hoped that the young lady pointing up her nose at them would one day think back on this night and realize that sexuality doesn't end at thirty or forty or fifty or sixty. At best, Carole could break the cycle; at worst, at least Carole was having a good time with Brick on the scant dance floor.

Joel and Sue meanwhile made their own fun at the bar, playing quarters with a group of frat guys who preferred to stay on campus with easy access to booze than to be at home with their suburban families. One of the Alpha Deltas made eyes at Joel, and it made him feel more alive than he had all year.

The frat guy bounced his quarter on the wooden bar counter but missed the cup.

"Fuck!" he shouted.

"Sure, but usually the guy buys me dinner first," Joel flirted.

"Black Velvet" is a five-minute song, and until the last few chords, the group of friends forgot about their troubles. They didn't think about naughty or nice, they didn't concern themselves with the waiting reindeer near the dumpster, and they certainly didn't consider their ages or status among the crowd. The three friends were content for what felt like the first time in all their lives.

Of course, it didn't last long. Alannah Myles ended and some new Lizzo song came on that reminded them all of their age. Joel knew some of the lyrics because of the spin class he took twice a week, but otherwise they were at a loss. It was their cue to regroup with the bartender.

"Three lemon drops," Sue said.

"Make that four," Carole corrected, ordering one for her new friend, Brick.

The bartender came back with four shots of well vodka, four lemon wedges, and four sugar packets.

"Wait, these aren't mixed," Sue said.

"We mix them ourselves," Joel added.

"What's the order? Suck the lemon, lick the sugar, then take the shot?" Brick asked.

"I think it's sugar, lemon, shot," Joel said.

"No, it's sugar, *make out*, shot, lemon," Carole replied confidently as she stared deeply into Brick's brown eyes.

Joel and Sue looked at each other, worried Carole might be having a little too much fun. They'd seen this side of her before, the Carole who made up for lost time by being the wildest version of herself. Before they could stop her, she poured the sugar packet on the back of her hand, licked it, tongue kissed Brick so hard, he turned to gravel, and then chased it with her lemon wedge while the others simply took the booze in and sucked on their lemon. It was too late, so they figured they might as well join the party.

"Merry Christmas!" Carole exclaimed as the liquor traveled down her throat. "I gotta run to the bathroom."

"I'll come with," Sue said, chasing her friend on the way to the dive bar restroom, their cheap shoes sticking to the dirty baseboard with every step.

Once inside, Sue started rummaging through her purse while Carole started fixing her hair.

"I can't find my—"

"Isn't it a relief you're not going to finish that sentence with *tampon*?"

"Found it!" Sue said, pulling out a small ziplock bag filled with cocaine she'd had in there since the Cher concert she and Joel went to. "You up for a little booger sugar?"

"Let it snow!" Carole replied.

After a few lines, the gals exited the bathroom and met Joel and Brick at the bar.

"You girls ready to go home?" Joel asked.

"Joel, you better get some caffeine in you because we just

recharged our batteries for a long night ahead," Sue said, casually thumbing her own nose to indicate what she and Carole had done while away.

"Bartender, vodka Red Bull, please!" Joel instructed.

"If I were a bettin' man, I'd say you three couldn't handle an all-nighter," Brick challenged.

"You like bettin'?" Carole asked.

"I've been known to gamble a bit in my day, but no horse races or blackjack tables around these parts."

"Come with us," Carole said as she made her way to the door and signaled the others to follow. Joel chugged his drink, slapped the ass of the frat guy who'd given him the sexy eye, and ran toward Carole with Sue and Brick in tow.

"Where we going?" Sue asked.

"We're going to Vegas!" Carole said as she approached the reindeer.

"You sure we should do this, Carole? Why don't we take the sleigh back, and your hubby can at least get a bunch of the gifts delivered. Or we could deliver them ourselves! I'm sure there's an instruction manual..."

"Joel, I've put everyone ahead of me for my entire life, and it stops now. It's time for me to have a jolly Christmas."

The group landed in Las Vegas fifteen minutes later, in record time thanks to the magic of Comet and company. Carole had forgotten to bring cash or her ATM card, so they had to detour at a nearby pawn shop. They grabbed the big-ticket items from the toy sack and walked into a place called Quick

Pawn off the Strip. A man named Petey, with earrings and a ponytail filled with gray hair, welcomed them, eventually offering two thousand dollars for an assortment of video game systems and other child electronics. Joel thought they deserved at least thirty-five hundred, but Petey could tell they were in a hurry to get gambling and opted to take advantage.

Once inside Caesar's Palace, it was hard to tell it was Christmas Eve. They pump those rooms with so much oxygen, lighting, and sounds that it's impossible to distinguish what time of day it is for anyone seated at a slot machine. The group agreed to split the two thousand into five hundred dollars each, and then they planned on putting all winnings in a pot to go home. Brick immediately ghosted the group after getting his five hundred dollars. He was off to another location without telling the others, but Carole, Joe, and Sue didn't mind. Brick was simply a symptom of their holiday fever, and now that he was out of the picture, they weren't planning on missing him.

Carole lost her share in just a handful of rounds of fifty-dollar blackjack, while Joel wasted his on the *Wheel of Fortune* slots. Sue, on the other hand, had the luck of the Irish on her side, as she hit the jackpot on a four-leaf-clover slot machine. She won a car, but the casino let her decide if she would rather have the cash, so instead of a Honda, she left with thirty-six thousand dollars (after taxes).

"I can't believe I won! On Christmas! Should I donate this money to charity or something?" Sue asked, feeling guilty for winning so much off the gifts that were supposed to be for kids tucked in their beds at home.

"Absolutely not. We're blowing it all tonight on whatever we want," Carole said.

"Ya know, it *is* Christmas. Maybe it would be good to give some of this to the youths tonight," Joel suggested.

"You mean deliver cash to sleeping kids in the sleigh?" Carole asked.

"No…I wasn't thinking children, but I do know some young people who could use it…"

Next thing they knew, Carole, Sue, and Joel were at Gemstones, a strip club off the Strip with lots of youngish strippers. As they walked through the smoke-filled room, they noticed a familiar face in the corner getting a private dance. It was Brick with a woman named Amethyst. He looked happy, so they chose not to interrupt.

"Give 'em each a grand, and I'll get some toys for the moms!" Carole said as she walked back out to the sleigh to get the toy sack.

Inside the club, women named after gemstones danced for men of various ages. Joel and Sue went to each and handed them a stack of hundreds, while Carole dragged the sack into the back room and wrote a note on it. *Free toys for your kids.* Carole might not have wanted to deliver toys to all the children who were sleeping in their beds that night, but she felt like the kids of Jade, Ruby, and Aquamarine were more than worthy of everything they didn't pawn.

"Carole, it's four thirty a.m.! I gotta get home! My sister and her family are coming over for brunch," Sue said.

"I should get going too. I told my parents we'd go see the new Sandra Bullock movie," Joel added.

Carole wasn't quite satisfied, but she wanted to be a good friend. Lifelong friends are hard to find and even harder to maintain. This wild holiday night was the best "friendaissance" these three could've ever had. As Carole hugged Joel and Sue tight and said goodbye, her heart was fuller than the Grinch's after he decided not to steal Christmas.

Carole flew around the sky all alone in her husband's sleigh. She thought about her childhood, favorite Christmas Eves with her parents, waking up Christmas morning and seeing what Santa had left her, years before she entered a relationship with the man who'd taken over those duties. She remembered meeting Nick and later marrying him, standing alongside her best buds.

Carole flew back over Vegas, above the Strip, with Dasher, Dancer, and the others, looking down at all the colors and lights. As someone whose life is Christmas, she was used to seeing glowing strands of twinkle lights all around her, but they'd gotten dimmer over the years. Carole needed the neons of hotel names and attractions to recognize how dull her existence had become.

As Carole turned the sleigh around, the lit pink heart attached to the Elvis Marriage Chapel reminded her of something her mom had said to her on her wedding day as she fit her veil: "In long-term relationships, there are good years and bad years, and the bad are impossible to avoid. You must find someone who is worth the bad years."

Eventually, Carole made her way back to the North Pole

just as the sun was coming up on the West Coast. Nick was fast asleep on the living room couch as another rerun of *Shark Tank* played on the TV. Carole covered his bare feet with a blanket and kissed him on the forehead. The resentment and anger she had toward him drifted away as she saw him sleeping so peacefully, and the good years came swiftly into focus.

"Carole, you're home," Nick said, slowing fading into consciousness.

"Go back to sleep, honey," Carole said.

"Is it too late? Is it already morning?" he asked.

"Yes, it's too late for the presents, but it will all be okay."

"But what about the kids?"

"I gave out some toys, but don't worry about that. Life isn't always fair; kids need to learn that lesson. And we need to learn to prioritize our relationship by prioritizing ourselves. We can't help others unless we help ourselves first."

"I love you," he said.

"I love you too."

Carole and Nick started a new tradition that year, the tradition of not giving an eff and not following the path they had taken so routinely all those years prior. Of course, they didn't stop Christmas completely; they just decided to do it in a new way. Sometimes they hit only half the houses; others, more. Some years, Carole went down the chimneys herself, while others, Nick took the reins as Carole spent time with her best friends. The couple even spent a few December 24ths at Caesars Palace...together. Rather than stress when they didn't make it to a house or a neighborhood, they simply did the best they could to ensure they had more good years than bad. They *both* realized their marriage wouldn't last the way it was before.

Back in Nevada, a little girl named Ruby sprang out of bed and ran to the living room. There it was, the bedazzled karaoke microphone of her dreams. Her mom, Sapphire, had gotten home with just enough time to place it under the tree after working the late shift at Gemstones. Ruby and her mom played with their new toy all day long, singing and dancing like Bing Crosby and Danny Kaye.

Santa used to end his gig with one loud "merry Christmas to all, and to all a good night! Ho, ho, ho!" This year was a little different. Santa went back to dreamland as Carole drew herself a bath, poured a glass of wine, and applied the moisturizing eye patches she kept in the vegetable drawer of the refrigerator. As she ran the bathwater, she noticed her husband's red velvet jacket on the vanity chair, the one he hadn't gotten to wear to deliver the presents the night before. She caressed the soft material, and a drop of her pinot noir accidentally spilled on the sleeve. The dark red wine mixed with the fabric and gave it a new black coloring that reminded Carole of the wild night that was now a beautiful memory. Normally, she would've immediately patted down the stain, then cleaned and pressed it for next year to ensure it wasn't permanent. Instead, Carole grabbed her phone, opened Spotify, and pressed play on "Black Velvet" by Alannah Myles. As the familiar chords started, she texted her besties...

Merry Christmas to me, I had a great fucking night.

Parents Weekend

The leaves fall every October on the gorgeously landscaped green of Ohio University, the setting of our next unfortunately true story. It's a quaint college town straight out of a Nancy Meyers movie. Exposed brick adorns the architecture, and local businesses line Court Street, where students descend every year to buy their schoolbooks. It's where I spent my first two years of college and home to one of the biggest Halloween parties in the country. In such a *Gilmore Girls*-esque town filled with artisanal coffee shops and young adults fighting the Ohio chill with oversize sweatshirts, it's shocking to see nearly thirty thousand partygoers dressed like Austin Powers and promiscuous nurses every October 31. The beauty of Ohio University is the yin and the yang of the town. It's cozy and beautiful yet filled with debaucherous students drinking like fish. I'm talking the biggest boozers in the world. I've never seen humans drink the way they do in Athens, Ohio.

College and drinking go together like mac and cheese. Young people are finally free from the shackles of their parents and surrounded by coeds their age who are all looking to socialize. They have four-ish years to do keg stands and power hours, theme parties and ice luges. Ohio University turns the hobby of drinking into a sport, and the students are some of the best alcohol athletes in the entire world.

Not only are the Halloweens wild, but there are various other weekends that are strictly boozing holidays. Street festivals where your entire job is to black out and family weekends where relatives and loved ones come to visit, stay in the dorms, and wake up without a memory of the night before. Many of the students come from a long line of Ohio University grads, so the parents get to arrive in Athens and relive their youth on these special occasions. They drink as much as if not more than their kids, and you often see moms falling down the stairs, dads hitting on their kid's friends, and bar tabs reaching the high heavens. My parents, Linda and Gary, visited together my sophomore year and couldn't quite hang like some of their contemporaries.

Mom and Dad drove down on a Saturday afternoon from their Cleveland suburb. Dad had a green-and-white football jersey, and Mom brought me fall word art to hang in my dorm: a wooden sign that listed autumnal buzzwords in various fonts. Pumpkin. Football. Patch. Grateful. Apples. Autumn. Leaves. Bonfire. Harvest. Pie. Sweater. Hot Cocoa. Hayrides. And in the center? Home.

"Dan, I brought you this for your room. A little slice of home for when you miss us," Mom said as she leaned the cheap frame against my combination microwave-refrigerator.

"So what kind of trouble are we getting into?" Dad asked.

"We missed the football game, but my roommates got a table at one of the places on Court Street, so we can meet them there and eat!"

"Should I change? What kind of restaurant is it?"

OU didn't really have restaurants, just dive bars that served pizza and a little buggy that made burritos until 2:00 a.m. That's about it. I lived with three straight guys who started drinking early with their folks, and I knew Gary and Linda wouldn't be able to imbibe for long, so it was a good thing we were running a bit behind the rest of our group. By the time we arrived at the bar, my friends had a booth and a handful of empty beer steins in front of them.

"Danny! Over here!" my roommate yelled when he saw us walk in the door.

I nodded and pulled my parents aside, away from the crowd. "Now, look, OU students can get a bit wild—"

"You think Mom and Dad are too square for your cool new friends, huh?" Dad said.

"No, I just want you to be prepared because a lot of the parents drink with their kids, and I know I'm not twenty-one, but—"

"I'll have a brewski with my son, no problem."

"Gary! He's underage!" Mom argued.

"I don't have to drink. I just wanted to tell you everyone else might be a little wild."

"Hold on, Dan. I think I got gum on my shoe," Mom said as she looked down at the underside of her Nina Wests.

"It's not gum. The floor is just sticky."

"Why would we go somewhere with a sticky floor?"

"Every place here has a sticky floor," I told her.

Mom didn't go to college, so she largely missed out on the experience of sticky bar flooring. She met my dad when she was eighteen, and they married before she even turned twenty-one. She was pregnant with my oldest brother when other people her age were walking to stage in their caps and gowns. My two older brothers went on to undergraduate learning, but their college experiences were a bit different from mine. They bypassed the dorms and went to a school that wasn't as isolated as Ohio University. My oldest brother didn't live on campus, and my middle brother played basketball, so he was usually traveling or practicing when other students were taking part in parents weekend or pledge week. My dad and I were the only ones who experienced a traditional college lifestyle.

When we sat with my friends and their parents, Dad fit right in with the crowd. He ordered a Blue Moon and started chatting everyone up like they were longtime besties.

"Can I get a glass of your house red over ice?" Mom asked the server as she took off her jacket.

As the drinks flowed, each mom began to tell the tales of their wild nights. To get to know each other, they shared intimate details about what they were like before parenting.

"I got so drunk one time, I woke up the next morning in the middle of a cornfield," Tonya said.

"That's nothing. I was so drunk one night, I ended up puking in the back of a cop car," Harriet added.

"My son better close his ears for this one, because one time during my junior year, I screwed the entire floor of a frat house. Five guys. Like the burger joint," Trish said.

Each mom story topped the previous, one-upping the others in their drunken glory. The only mom left at the table to tell a boozy tale was Linda Pellegrino. I tried to change the subject, knowing Mom probably didn't have anything as juicy as the others, but she chimed in over me to fit in with the crowd...

"Well, my Danster doesn't know this, but my husband, Gary, and I went to a wedding a while back, and my best friend, Chris, was at our table. Chris went to the bar, and she came back with *two* drinks. She said, Lin, I got you a drink. It's called a Long Island iced tea.' I thought it was like Lipton! So I took one sip, and then I immediately turned to my husband and said, Gar, we have got to go. And then we left. Before they even did cake!"

Everyone at the table's eyes lingered on my mom, waiting for the rest of her story, but she was done. There was no rest of the story. That was it. A wise prophet (Kathie Lee Gifford) once said that everyone has a story, and Linda's ended with a car ride home and a mostly full Long Island iced tea that was not, in fact, like the Lipton she was used to.

As time goes on, I find myself morphing into my parents and even inheriting some stray qualities from the generation prior. I fold gently used tinfoil to use later like Grandma Rose, I swear like Dad, and I quite often find myself being fully satisfied with just one glass of red over ice like Mom.

Advent Calendar

BE CAREFUL WITH YOUR SEASONAL CANDLES. Learn from me. I haven't always practiced caution when it comes to my pine three-wicks. In fact, I once lit my kitchen on fire, so let this next story be a cautionary tale.

It was an unusually hot California December, one that made me miss the cozy comforts of the Midwest. The sun is beautiful, but sometimes I long for the snowy landscapes of Ohio. California living is also insanely expensive. I've lived in a lot of small places, including my last apartment, which was technically a one-bedroom but might as well have been a studio. The kitchen/office/living room were all one. My little desk was up against a wall, and I had a two-person high-top dining table right behind it. The space was small and quaint, but I was proud of the little home I paid for all by myself.

I even saved up enough to buy some fancy decorations for the holidays. Specifically, I went ham on the Chip and Joanna Magnolia home collection at Target due to that weekend binge of *Fixer Upper* while I was hungover. The farmhouse trend has since been overdone, and though I never want to see shiplap again, I was very into it for a short period of my life, which led me to buy a bunch of their merch: wreaths, plaid green place mats, and cute wrapping paper for gifts. That same year, I also purchased a Yankee Candle advent calendar. Every day in December, in anticipation of Christmas, I would unwrap a new votive from the calendar, each one a different scent for the holidays.

Although the candles were tiny, it was so fun to wake up each day and find a new wick to burn; scents like balsam, cedar, Christmas wish, and holiday hearth made up the package. I set each day's candle in the middle of my Magnolia Home tablescape and got to work at my li'l office near the table where they flamed.

Working from home has always worked out well for me; I have a flexible schedule and make my own lunches. Occasionally, I treat myself to food delivery or sneak away for a quick midday workout. One especially busy day, I had a turkey sandwich—wrapped in brown paper with a pickle spear on the side—delivered from a nearby deli I loved. Since my table was covered with my new decor and I was busy, I ate my food at the desk. In fact, I was so busy that I didn't get up to throw away my trash. I simply tossed the packaging over my shoulder during a phone call and watched out of the corner of my eye as it landed on the table. What I didn't realize at that moment was that the trash landed on the lit candle, causing the brown paper to light on fire, a fire that spread to the other new items I bought courtesy of Chip and Joanna.

I was on the phone and facing my computer, so I didn't realize right away that my kitchen was on fire—and with a scented candle, the smell was cozy rather than alarming. Instead of burning, I was overwhelmed with a scent called Dickens. It was a spicy aroma of cinnamon, cloves, nutmeg, and something fruity, apparently inspired by Charles Dickens, author of *A Christmas Carol.* I'm not sure why the candle company thinks they know what Charles Dickens's house smelled like, but they did their best to recreate it. Knowing the publishing industry, it was likely Chuck wrote *A Christmas Carol* in June the previous year so he could make his fourth-quarter release date.

By my calculations, that would mean the Dickens scent should be more cucumber melon than Christmassy. Regardless, by the time I noticed the fire, it was too late. Maybe that's poor phrasing because the apartment building survived, but my Magnolia Home holiday collection did not. The plaid place mats oddly held up perfectly even though they were cloth, but the rest of my decorations were ruined, burned to a crisp.

(Here's a photo of some of the damage. I was cleaning up wax and ashes for months.)

I was so distraught from my kitchen fire that I had to get out of the house, so I went for a hike at Runyon Canyon, a popular trail that leads to the top of a mountain overlooking Los Angeles. On my walk, I thought about how lucky I was to catch the fire before it spread because I don't know what I would've done if I had burned down the whole building. The endorphins from the walk started to mix with the adrenaline, and I began to laugh at the whole ordeal. I survived an advent-calendar holiday fire!

Once I reached the top of the hill, I decided to do what every millennial does when a life event happens: I went live on Instagram to be dramatic. Overlooking the city, I said hello to my followers and all the people who joined in to watch what I had to say in the middle of the day.

"Wow. I am here, midday, to let you all know about the tragedy I just experienced. Like Reba McEntire once sang in the theme song to her hit show *Reba,* I'm a survivor. I narrowly escaped a near-death experience of open flames..."

I was laying it on thick to make light of the situation. Of course, it was a simple candle fire, and no one was hurt, so I thought it was especially funny that I was acting like the situation was a near-death experience! I was being cheeky! My face was stern as I recounted the open flames while the city of Los Angeles acted as my backdrop. Unfortunately, what I didn't realize was that much more serious events were unfolding behind me.

"Holy shit, is that your place?"

"Omigod, Danny! Are you okay?"

"This is so scary, stay safe!"

These were just a few of the comments rolling in fast and furious from people following my Instagram Live. I assumed they were playing along with me, overdramatizing for laughs. Little did I know there was an actual, real, very scary fire happening over my shoulder.

Growing up in the Midwest, we feared tornadoes and thunderstorms, but California must contend with wildfires, which spread quickly and furiously—just like the one happening at that exact moment. I looked behind me and saw the smoke filling the LA air, billowing up to the clouds. Quickly, I clicked END and got off Instagram to avoid any more confusion. Here was a whole city on fire, and I was harping on and on about a candle that burned some items I got from Target in my shitty apartment.

Texts started coming through from friends who'd seen my live.

Are you okay? Was that your house on fire in the background?

Please tell me you're fine, I saw part of your live! You said your place was on fire? It looked bad!

You made it out okay? Are you staying safe on the mountain?

People thought I was talking about the wildfires instead of my Dickens candle! Too many people had seen the video. I had to do something! I began texting everyone back, trying to explain I was joking and didn't realize there was a wildfire behind me.

I just heard, you okay?

Call me!

Word was getting to people who hadn't even seen my live; they had just heard about it from others. Social media drama can spread quicker than fanned flames, and it was happening in real time. My only option was to get back on Instagram Live to explain myself.

"Heyyyyy, guys, so I'm back. I hope I didn't scare everyone before. Um, I, um, didn't realize there was a wildfire happening. I had, uh, a little kitchen fire earlier with my Dickens advent-calendar candle, which spread to some seasonal Magnolia Home merch, but I'm okay, and, um, uh, the fire I was talking about was not the same as the one happening behind me. It was just, like, a little joke fire. I missed the news, so I didn't know there was a serious one. I'm sorry for the confusion, and, uh, hopefully everyone is okay. Stay safe out there! Okay, um, bye!"

Just last week, I saw an old friend who asked what it was like to live through my house burning down. They hadn't seen my follow-up video, so they'd just assumed I set an apartment building on fire. It was my first experience apologizing publicly, and I hope it's my last. One thing it did teach me is that social media is a whole lot of smoke and mirrors, sometimes literally. Now whenever I'm at the store and see a holiday candle scent called Dickens, I think not only of the cloves and spice but the smell of regret and embarrassment.

Last-Minute Gift Idea: WEED

THIS IS A FAMILY-FRIENDLY BOOK! I'm certainly not saying one should gift another person drugs for the high holy holiday...but I am implying it. Okay, this isn't really a family book per se. It is explicit, and if *The Jolliest Bunch* were an album, it would have one of those parental advisory stickers on the cover...because this is meant for adults. Specifically, it's written for gays and women, although I know there are a lot of straight men sneaking their copies under the covers with a flashlight. On my last book tour, each venue had a minimum of six straight men, who were the best of all the straight men because they were comfortable and confident enough to be in a crowd of women and gays. I see you boys, and I love you!

Anyway, drugs are bad. We know that. But sometimes the healthy ones can be a nice holiday gift idea! I'm specifically talking about weed. You can get someone a sensible (legal) joint or a peppermint edible. Who doesn't need a little marijuana to escape the stress of the end of the year?

Through high school and college, I steered clear of just about everything drug related. My friends and I liked to get drunk off wine coolers when someone's parents were out of town, but it was always a safe environment filled with group dancing and snacks. Inevitably, the rest of the group would pair off and start making out, and that's when I'd cut off the boozing and head on over to those grocery store sprinkle cookies.

Speaking of processed foods, I already told you about my bad high, when I accidentally ate expired body products from Jessica Simpson's line of goods. One time, I also fortuitously emailed my primary care physician after watching a season-six holiday episode of *Full House* stoned. On the episode, one of the Tanner girls got a Candy Land board game under the tree. Somehow, I remembered Candy Land playing a part in an earlier episode and decided to email myself this fun trivia fact.

The autofill on my email client sent the message to my doctor instead of me, so Dr. D. got an email that said:

> In Season 5, episode 14 of Full House Michelle is playing candy land, but in season 6 episode 12, a very Tanner Christmas episode—there's candy land under tree. She's getting a gift she already owns!

Dr. D. responded with:

> Hi Danny!
> Hope you had a nice thanksgiving. haven't seen either.
> -Dr. D.

Oops. Despite my negative experiences, I do want to recommend marijuana as a gift idea! Here's why:

Before my big brother Bryan had kids and responsibilities, I got him high for Christmas. Specifically, I gave him a weed brownie, then told him to eat a quarter of it and sit his ass in front of the TV where I had one of his favorite movies ready (*Old School*). While he was watching Will Ferrell and company, I ran out for the rest of his gift. Edibles usually take about an hour to kick in, so I had some time to drive to every nearby fast-food place.

When I got back to the condo we shared, I set all the food on the table and called my big brother into the kitchen. His munchies were strong, and I had all his faves:

- McDonald's French fries
- Wendy's cheeseburger
- Garlic parmesan wings from Buffalo Wild Wings
- Taco Bell taco
- Arby's beef and cheddar
- Dairy Queen soft serve vanilla with crunch coat on for dessert

The gift was a hit! He made his way through the six-course meal in record time and sat back down to finish the movie.

They say experiences make the best gifts, so this year, give someone the experience of the perfect munchies. Fast food is cheap and quick and makes a perfect companion to the stoner experience.

Detour

No one asked, but I thought we could take a little detour for my personal grown-up Christmas list!

Dear Santa,

Peace on earth, racial equity, equal pay for women, and LGBTQ+ rights are on my list, but you haven't done those yet, so I'm assuming you aren't going to. We'll skip ahead to the other stuff...

- ☞ Remember those fake-healthy granola bars called Kudos that had things like M&M's and Snickers mixed in? They're discontinued, and I need you to bring them back.
- ☞ Please convince Rihanna to go back to releasing new albums every year.
- ☞ I want Alfre Woodard to be a huge star. Like the kind of success those Chrises (Evans, Hemsworth, etc.) get. Specifically, I want her to be able to get any project she wants greenlit. Whether she wants to play a superhero, a detective, a sex addict, a person who hates sex, a princess, a rock star, a protagonist in a reboot of *Carol* with Loretta Devine...give her whatever she wants.
- ☞ Stop with the price tags on HomeGoods/TJ Maxx items.
- ☞ I want those sparkling waters to last longer. Specifically, to not get flat after three minutes of being opened. I always feel like it's a race against the clock every time I open a La Croix because they don't taste as good when they aren't fizzing.
- ☞ Give Bonnie Hunt the proper starring vehicle. Same with Judy Greer. Maybe put them together in something.
- ☞ Reboot Jonathan Taylor Thomas.
- ☞ There should be a *Home Alone* spinoff for Buzz's girlfriend (woof).

Holidays with the A-Group

Did you get a senior superlative in high school? Best Dressed, Most Likely to Succeed, or Biggest Slacker? I was voted Most Involved and Best Personality by my graduating class because I was doing it all and doing it all with a smile! Class president, drama, Key Club (whatever that was)...I signed up for any and everything they would let me. I even lettered in student council. Most people think you can only get a letterman jacket for things like football or track, but I'm here to tell you that you can also get one for varsity student council. I'd like to think I was leading the student body for the right reasons, but I probs was just doing all the school clubs to avoid sex. While my peers were busy making out, I was suppressing my sexuality by planning prom and meeting with the principal to discuss vending machine snack options. As class president, I was always trying to think of new activities, charity events, fundraisers, and adventures that would keep me hanging out with girls while not being expected to physically touch them.

During my time in office, I got to attend leadership conferences out of state and hobnob with other student leaders from schools across the country, giving me a front-row seat to the saga of two chaotic young Ohioan women named Brooklyn and Chrissy.

Brooklyn was part of the A-group, not only within her district but within the county, the state, the world! Okay, maybe not quite the world, but a lot of people knew of Brooklyn's accomplishments—her quarterback boyfriend, the Benz her parents bought her to drive around town, her chihuahua named Daisy whom she treated like an accessory. There was even a rumor that she'd won some pageant called Miss Teen Ohio Galaxy Girl, which I don't think was a real thing? She was the Regina George, the trendsetter, an influencer, the queen bee! For a minute during the Obama administration, it felt like schools were ridding themselves of the archaic social hierarchy that plagued students for centuries, but I have young nieces and nephews who tell me that all went out the window and the social standings are back in vogue.

Cliques look different than they used to, but there's *always* going to be some asshole running things and making lives hell. Brooklyn was that girl when I was a teen. I once heard her insult another girl by telling everyone that she bought her socks online. Like, that was the entire insult, and it worked because of Brooklyn's ruthless delivery. A young lady chose to cover her hooves with e-commerce, and apparently that was a bad thing. I haven't stopped thinking about it since and certainly have never turned to Amazon for socks. Did you ever see that movie *Georgia Rule* with Lindsay Lohan and Jane Fonda? Jane plays Georgia, and she has all these odd rules that everyone has to follow. Brooklyn is the Georgia, and she made the rules, number one of which was no online socks.

Chrissy was Brooklyn's number two—a girl next door, still wildly popular, gorgeous, and smart—but she didn't have the wealth Brooklyn had and was forever self-conscious about it. They even looked alike; the only real difference was that Chrissy cut her hair short to stand out, and her budget hairstylist didn't do her any justice. It just made Brooklyn's luscious long locks look even better in comparison. For their school, hierarchy had less to do with looks and more to do with dollar signs, so Brooklyn didn't shade Chrissy's hair; she shaded the cheap stylist who did it. No matter how many people liked Chrissy more than Brooklyn, she always felt not quite good enough because she couldn't afford the Chanel bags and stylists. The two girls were best frenemies, but their school knew Brooklyn was the queen bee and class president to Chrissy's vice.

One thing Brooklyn and Chrissy did share...a father. Here's where the story gets twisted and Shakespearean. Brooklyn's mom and Chrissy's mom each slept with a guy named David when they were in high school, and David fathered both their children. Brooklyn and Chrissy were half sisters, but no one ever *really* knew the details of the complicated family tree. It was this weird open secret that people whispered about but didn't dare mention in their presence.

You might be wondering what was so great about this David that enabled him to get with half the school's parents. The only things David really had going for him were his abs and a trust fund, but in high school, that was enough to make him a prize to be won. David knocked up the two gals during their senior year and ended up settling down with Brooklyn's mom. Meanwhile, Chrissy was raised by her single mother, who had too much pride for David's child support checks.

Brooklyn lived a lavish lifestyle off her dad's inheritance. They had a huge house, a beautifully landscaped yard, and a live-in housekeeper-chef, while Chrissy and her mom (still single) lived in a modest house in the same town and shopped discount. Brooklyn and Chrissy knew they were half sisters—this wasn't a *The Parent Trap* situation—but the family dynamics always caused underlying tension. That tension spilled over into the rest of the A-group, the group of friends that surrounded Brooklyn and Chrissy and included a boy named Thomas and a girl named Laney, whose real name was Aslan (like the lion from *The Chronicles of Narnia*). I always thought it was strange that someone with a name as cool as Aslan would go by Laney, but I digress. Brooklyn would throw fancy parties at her house for the A-group; Chrissy wouldn't dare have friends over.

You might be wondering how the moms handled this social hierarchy. I was. I got to spend some time with Chrissy's mom at a bake sale, and she was *obsessed* with her daughter's standing, obviously still harboring resentment toward Brooklyn's parents as she watched them live out the life she wanted. "Chrissy lets Brooklyn be in charge, but she's more of a natural leader," she told me. They were two generations of frenemies living in the same Midwest town and pouring all those family dynamics into student council activities.

Junior year is especially important for high school students because college applications are around the corner, and many students are fighting for acceptance into a good college. When you don't have rich parents who can bribe your way into school, you rely on things like a résumé and grades, which is why that year was a turning point for Chrissy. She wanted to give up her number two spot and become the head of the A-group, determined to get into a better school than Brooklyn, and that desire led to a holiday charity showdown that ended with Brooklyn set on fire.

So where do I fit into all this, and how do I know all the intricate details of the web these young ladies weaved? Enter Thomas. Thomas was part of the A-group, one of the minions who worshipped Brooklyn and Chrissy. He was openly gay, which in 2002ish in Ohio was very brave and out of the ordinary. I wouldn't come out until I was twenty-two, but that didn't stop me from occasionally kissing Thomas after meeting him at a StuCo (slang for *student council*) conference. Although I mentioned earlier that I was avoiding sex in high school, I *did* make out with Thomas once every three months during my junior year, something that felt safe since he didn't go to my school. It was our little secret, and I'd usually only see him when Brooklyn and Chrissy were around anyway. Those two were so busy with their rivalry that they wouldn't even notice when Thomas and I snuck off into an empty room somewhere for a little first base action (I was too scared to go further than that). All that backstory brings us to pre–winter break of 2002.

JC Chasez's bandmate once said, "What's better than a million dollars? A billion dollars." And what's better than doing charity for one end-of-year holiday? Doing charity for *all* the end-of-year holidays. That was what Brooklyn and Chrissy set out to do that year in their battle for the number one spot. Brooklyn would have an idea, and then Chrissy would try to one-up it, ultimately snowballing into a full calendar of events. They organized a Christmas toy drive, they went to a predominantly Jewish nursing home to light menorahs for Hanukkah, and they served meals to homeless people downtown for Turkey Day. I tried to keep up at my school, but it was impossible. They were being too charitable! And I didn't have the money Brooklyn did, so she did it all better. Her toy drive had presents wrapped impeccably with expensive Hallmark wrapping paper, while ours were delivered unwrapped. For the food bank, she hired expensive caterers to feed everyone fancy meals, while I was ready to serve whatever slop they had on hand. I learned at an early age that it's impossible to compete with rich people. That also resulted in Brooklyn taking credit for almost every event because Chrissy couldn't front the cash like her half sister could.

Since I couldn't compete at my school, I offered to lend a hand with their activities, which also gave me an excuse to see Thomas. Things officially got out of hand when Brooklyn, a young white woman, showed up at a tree lighting wearing a homemade kente cloth. It's a traditional African garb that she thought was appropriate for Kwanzaa, but she added a belt to cinch the waist and some cutouts to show off her ample bosom. It was *Sex and the City 2* before Carrie and the gang spent a hundred and forty minutes in Abu Dhabi. The public's awareness of cultural appropriation has come a long way, but even back in the early aughts, we knew not to be Brooklyn. Deep down, I think she even knew that it was inappropriate, but she had her other blond white girlfriends in the A-group wear the same. Thomas narrowly escaped the wardrobe because he and I were dry humping when the girls were at the fabric store.

At the tree lighting, I had a tiny table setup where I was selling hot chocolate with a small group of kids from my school, and I wish I could say we were collecting money for a charity or our prom fund, but I think we wound up using it to go see *The Santa Clause 2* in theaters. There was a stage near the tree where the mayor was going to say hello, welcome the townsfolk, and then hit a button that would light the tree and start the music. All standard fare, except somehow Brooklyn weaseled her way onto the stage *with* the mayor. I have no doubt it was all an effort to write on her college applications that she "was in charge of the town tree lighting in conjunction with the mayoral office."

Detour

Our town did something called Teen Court, where petty crimes would be tried like an actual courthouse. I volunteered to be on the jury, deciding how much community service a fourteen-year-old would get when she stole a Martina McBride CD from the local Kmart. I used that credit on my apps as "legal counsel," so I couldn't fault Brooklyn for her work with the local government.

"Welcome to the tree lighting! The holiday season is upon us, and this year, local high school student Brooklyn is going to help me do the honors with a special all-inclusive message," the mayor said to a festive crowd.

"Hello! I'm Brooklyn, and it's so important to help around the holidays, which is why we're collecting money in the THS booth over there. So often, other holidays get pushed to the background in December, so I wanted to take a moment to honor all our end-of-year holidays, which is why I'm wearing an authentic kente cloth for Kwanzaa and will guide us in a Jewish prayer as I light a menorah."

The rest of the A-group was scattered throughout the event. Thomas was waiting in a bathroom stall for me at a nearby Panera, Aslan was manning the collections table, and Chrissy was just offstage dreaming of standing in front of the crowd like Brooklyn was. If Chrissy would've taken time to write Santa a letter that year, she would've asked for the life Brooklyn had, for her mother to marry David, for the school quarterback to be her date to prom instead of Brooklyn's. Most importantly, Chrissy would've asked for Brooklyn to be number two, so Chrissy could finally be queen bee.

Brooklyn stood in front of a small suburb of people, wearing the slutty kente cloth and holding a menorah, even though the only other Festival of Lights she had ever attended was World of Color at Disneyland. She motioned for Chrissy to join her onstage with the lighter, and Chrissy attempted to set flame to the menorah but instead accidentally lit Brooklyn's African tube top on fire. It was the smallest of flames, but Brooklyn freaked out. An elderly gentleman was right up front with his wife, who had just bought hot chocolate from me. He instinctively grabbed his wife's hot cocoa and doused Brooklyn with it to blow out the flame, only it didn't blow it out; it made things worse. The woman had spiked her hot chocolate with booze, and Brooklyn burst into even bigger flames like Nicolas Cage in *Ghost Rider*...

Just kidding about that last part. The old lady didn't actually spike her cocoa. Spiritually, I like to think she was imagining it was mixed with peppermint schnapps, but it was just chocolate. Regardless, it was still hot, sticky, and thick, and now it covered Brooklyn. Brooklyn ran offstage like a bat outta hell, and that was it for her holiday charity. The crowd watched in horror as this beautiful young mean girl was Carrie-d in front of the wintry crowd, only instead of pig's blood, she was doused with hot cocoa. As I watched in horror from the table where we gathered funds to see a Tim Allen movie, I noticed Chrissy's face. For a split second, I saw a gleam in her eye, and the sides of her mouth curled upward. I'm not saying Chrissy purposefully lit Brooklyn's offensive attire on fire, but I do think she was less than careful as she lit the candle.

The following year, Brooklyn gave up all her extracurriculars and fell into the arms of her boyfriend, Rock. She and Chrissy had a falling out, and Brooklyn spent her final year of high school with her other A-group friends like Thomas (whom I continued to hook up with sporadically for a decade), Aslan, and a new friend...lady MDMA, a mistress that came courtesy of her expendable funds that were no longer tied up doing school charity work.

Chrissy meanwhile took over as class president and got into a nice state school on scholarship. Despite spending twelfth grade with ecstasy, Brooklyn still got into the college she wanted. She never had to get involved or do any charity in the first place because of one thing: her family was rich. Rich people don't have to work hard or give back or be kind. They play by their own rules, and money talks louder than any bullet point on a résumé. I wish I could end this tale by telling you Brooklyn ended up with a shitty life or some sort of late-in-life comeuppance, but she married a hot doctor, looks younger than ever (according to social media), and had her kids young, so she's the hot mom. Last I heard, she was running the PTA, and I hope when she's helping plan holiday events, she remembers to do it for the greater good and to steer clear of open flames.

Midnight Mass

"Tell Grandma we all went to
midnight mass last night."

—MOM, EVERY CHRISTMAS MORNING

We didn't usually go to midnight mass. Sometimes Mom just wanted us to lie so we didn't look like heathens in the eyes of my extra-Catholic grandparents. I'd say we averaged about once every three years. The last time we all made it, it was after a Christmas Eve party where everyone stayed late. The final guest left around 11:59, and Mom corralled us into a car to get there, even though we were all either exhausted, tipsy, or both. When we arrived a few minutes late, the place was packed, and all five Pellegrinos had to find a seat at the back of the church—in a location where you can't see the priest and you can barely hear what he's saying over a half-working loudspeaker. Every other word of the service would cut out, so mass sounded something like, “Hail Mary…full of…fruit… amen.”

We took our seats and, one by one, closed our eyes. None of us got a chance to taste communion that year, but we did all get some much-needed sleep and finally got to see the priest up close when he woke us up after the service.

“Wake up!” he shouted.

Santa Claus may see you while you’re sleeping and know when you’re awake, but so does Father John. Personally, I believe Jesus wants you to practice self-care and get plenty of rest, so get that shut-eye, whenever and wherever you can. Amen.

Detour

Why does it feel like priests never age? You know how Dame Maggie Smith has been playing an elderly woman for over three decades? She first played an octogenarian in *Hook* back in 1991, then Mother Superior in the *Sister Act* movies, which happened decades before she checked into *The Best Exotic Marigold Hotel* or ruled the world of *Downton Abbey*. I feel like the clergy I grew up with were and still are whatever age Maggie Smith has been for all these years. DROP THE SKINCARE ROUTINE, FATHERS.

Text Me Merry Christmas

Merry Christmas! xoxo

Two words and two letters can mean so many different things when they're showing up on a fully charged phone December 25. It's the infamous holiday text, the one that comes through on your family group chat or from your coworker Natalie or from the guy you met at the local bar the night before whose name you have saved as *Zack Thick Hand.* I got acupuncture back in 2013, and the specialist still sends me a message every year with a still frame of the bird lady from *Home Alone 2.* Most people send a simple emoji or even a GIF, but Susan the acupuncturist opts for one promotional image of character actress Brenda Fricker. I wish I could tell you Susan sends me a graphic of the character smiling and saying, "Happy Holidays," but it's literally just a close-up of the pigeon lady with birds around her neck staring deeply into the camera with a grimace. *Feliz Navidad, Susan!* I write back to her annually. I must've mentioned the character during my last visit, so it's become a bad inside joke, even though I don't really know anything about Susan other than she stuck needles in my skin one year. I can't judge because I'm the crazy person who brought up the seasonal sequel side character in conversation with a woman I had just met, surely wanting to discuss how she was technically the female lead while Susan curbed my anxiety with needles.

All this is to say that I'm an expert in the holiday text, which is why I'm going to provide some ways to spruce up that SMS. Susan's impulse to send the pigeon lady was actually spot on in a lot of ways because the first rule of holiday texting is that you need to personalize with an attachment. People are especially lazy when it comes to this. I often notice that they will search "xmas" and attach the first GIF that shows up. It's usually Will Ferrell as Buddy the Elf squatting with his hands between his knees like he's gotta piss and wearing a big smile on his face. Nothing wrong with Buddy—we love that big elf—but enough. It's not personal. And neither is that generic snowman GIF with the sunglasses on it. Give a little pizzazz! Find a movie or TV show that the receiver knows is specific to you. My lesbian friend likes to send an image of Rooney Mara from the indie drama *Carol* starring her and Cate Blanchett. The moment I see Rooney wearing a Santa hat on my phone, I know my buddy Leslie is three glasses of pinot noir deep at her dad's house. When I reach out to my old college bestie Michelle on the big day, I like to send a clip of that *Saved by the Bell* holiday episode where Zack invites an unhoused man to live with him because he wants to hook up with his daughter (we should explore that episode some other time), while my buddy Beth gets a reminder of that time Teresa Giudice tossed her sister's sprinkle cookies in the garbage on *The Real Housewives of New Jersey*. If you're not a pop culture junkie, simply attach a selfie next to your passed-out aunt or a video of you and your drunk grandpa. It makes it more meaningful!

There are some exceptions to this attachment rule, namely if you're sending a text to a crush. You could still go with one of the aforementioned suggestions, but I think it's best to go with a simple smiling selfie instead of an attached image of a fictional character. Just make sure you're not too drunk, and if you're sipping wine, make sure you don't have a wine smile that makes you look like the Joker. We all get the pitter-patters when a text from a crush comes through, and I think often people try too hard to make it something super clever or witty. Or people overplay the sarcasm, and it just ends up coming across as mean. One time, a guy I liked sent me *you can't afford to eat as many cookies as Santa* with a picture of Saint Nick eating some snickerdoodles, and it emotionally broke me. He was trying to neg me, but it just left a sour taste in my mouth. Of course, we casually dated through Valentine's Day because that's who I am, but I broke it off as soon as Target put their candy hearts on clearance. If you like someone, just be simple and kind; it will mean the world to the receiver.

Punctuation, spelling, font—these are all important in crafting this once-a-year message. I'm a stickler for spelling, so make sure you aren't writing *Mary Christmas!* although I think it's okay to write *Merry Xmas!* which reads as less formal and less religious. I also prefer the *xo* to be uniform, so I will ignore my phone's suggestion of capitalizing the *x* in favor of a simple *xoxo*. An emoji shows you used a bit more effort, so include a heart or tree or both! Certain phones have options like confetti on the screen or making the words look bigger, but I think those take things a little too far and make it look less clean.

Ultimately, none of this matters as much as the person you're sending a message to, so be sure to curate your crowd throughout the year. Surround yourself with the kind of people who will write you and whom you want to reach out to. If you know that someone you love is spending the day alone or struggling with the season, be sure to message them first. This time of year can be incredibly lonely and isolating, so take care of each other. Good people are hard to come by, so don't take them for granted. A text takes just a few seconds and can really make someone's day.

If I had all your phone numbers, I would text you myself, but instead I leave you with this...

Holiday Ham

Food is extra important to Italians. We like to eat. A lot. And ensuring holiday meals are super special is a custom my people don't take lightly. It doesn't even have to technically be a special occasion; we'll make it one by cooking a whole lot of grub. Normal Sunday meals are cooked all day long, simmered and stirred with fresh ingredients and a keen eye. Grandma Rose used to spend all morning making her sauce and meatballs, we'd go eat and spend hours sitting around a dinner table chowing down, and that was just a regular ole day. Thanksgiving, Christmas, Easter...these are extra, super, big-deal, special kinds of meals. On Turkey Day, Mom sets her alarm for 4:00 a.m. so she can get up and start cooking. Nothing beats the scent of Mom's stuffing while Clay Aiken performs "Silver Bells" atop a Hershey's chocolate float. When I told my parents I was writing a holiday book, they assumed it was going to be filled with recipes—classics like my grandma's sugar cookies, Aunt Diane's pistachio pudding, and Mom's city chicken—because

Pellegrinos know how to cook, and food is of the utmost importance in relation to November/December.

There are also the seasonal treats around the later calendar months that are very important—the pumpkin-flavored cookies, cakes, and pies, the gingerbread lattes. I'm basic when it comes to this stuff; I will happily stock the cupboard with anything I can find with a pumpkin on the packaging. And there's nothing I love more than getting that first PSL of the season; the smell of warm cinnamon and pumpkin mixed with hot espresso and topped with decadent whipped cream is everything. I also love the minty sweetness of a peppermint mocha, the luscious shards of candy cane floating atop the warm coffee. I really think there's something magical about a holiday coffee, cozying up in a luscious cable-knit sweater and gripping an extra-large mug that says *Candy Cane Wishes & Mistletoe Kisses* on it.

I know I've talked about this before, but *You've Got Mail* is my favorite movie, and it always seemed so aspirational to me, the way Tom Hanks and Meg Ryan would go to Starbucks and get their coffees. I don't often treat myself in the warmer months, but come fall and winter, I find my nearest coffee shop and pretend I'm Kathleen Kelly on the streets of Nora Ephron's New York City. I carry a book with me and sip on my overpriced coffee. I get to, for $5.95, live the fantasy I had when I watched that movie in 1999, escaping the current world as I dream walk through my rom-com mirage. My current dream is that perhaps one of you out there reading this right now is on a subway with a hot drink in one hand and my book in another, with a scarf wrapped around your neck and the perfect winter coat (which isn't something current but a worn-in jacket that has lived through a few years of cold fronts). I hope you feel like Tom or Meg and this book is your *Pride and Prejudice*. I may not have the skillful prose of Jane Austen, but I hope my words assist in the *You've Got Mail* fantasy.

Seasonal treats are also very superstitious for my Italian family. Sauerkraut on New Year's for good luck, grilled oranges covered in olive oil for fortune, a sip of holy water for peace, and a bite of anise for goodwill. I hated the anise, but Grandma Rose was adamant that I have at least a small nibble so my year ahead didn't go to shit. Come to think of it, I have skipped the anise every year after she passed, and life has been downhill ever since, so I'll be heading to the grocery store this December to pick some up. Did we all collectively forget to eat the anise these past few years? Is that what's been going on?

I live in California now while my family is all back in Ohio, and the hardest part of my move is missing the good food I grew up eating. Very early on in my West Coast living, I started to collect all my mom's recipes, calling her, FaceTiming in, and trying to get measurements for dishes she's spent her lifetime eyeballing without an exact science. I'd ask how much flour go in her dumplings, and she'd say, "A couple of handfuls." The amount of cayenne pepper in her chili is "a few heavy pinches," and she only knows how to make her cherry squares in large batches, so the first time I made them, I had enough to feed my entire apartment building. *A few heavy pinches* could mean a couple of teaspoons or four cups! These made-up measurements are not universal, so it's hard to tell exactly how much to use. The only way to get her recipes was to make sure she called me whenever she was making one of my faves, so I'd have to stop everything at 2:00 p.m. my time and follow along over the phone, asking her to put her pinches and handfuls into spoons and cups before mixing them into the bowl.

After years of this process, I was finally able to put together a makeshift cookbook of my childhood favorites, something I hope to publish one of these days. Most are very Midwest comfort foods, the kinds of dishes that are incredibly delectable and anything *but* healthy. We're talking bars and squares, cakes poked with Jell-O, and bakes filled with cheeses and bread crumbs. In my twenties, I looked down on these dishes in favor of wheatgrass and kale, but now I appreciate the amount of love that gets poured into these meals. It's comfort food for a reason, because they're soups and stews, salads with anything but lettuce, and powdered sugar–topped desserts that make you feel good when you eat them. They may not help you live longer, but who wants to be alive at a hundred and ten without ever enjoying the fine cuisine of a Midwestern?

All that's to say I take food very seriously and come from a long bloodline of people who do the same. One of the most important items of the season is Linda Pellegrino's baked ham. The brown-sugar glaze drips off the skin, and the meat is topped with juicy pineapple slices that adorn the pig via wooden toothpicks. The ham is cut into quarter-inch pieces and served alongside homemade lasagna. The meat tastes heavenly when mixed with a bit of Mom's pasta sauce—a rich, tomato-flavored concoction that's slow cooked with Italian herbs and simmered with homemade meatballs and sausage. *Delizioso!* Mom usually orders the spiral ham and glazes it herself, timing everything perfectly so it finishes just as the guests are arriving.

Last Christmas, my dad oversaw picking up the ham, and it didn't go according to plan. All hell broke loose.

"Gary, did you pick up my ham at Mazzulo's?"

"No, I will," Dad replied.

"You were supposed to pick it up yesterday. I need to baste it."

Dad knew not to argue, so he hopped in his car and headed to what he thought was Mazzulo's. Unfortunately, he doesn't do much of the grocery shopping, so when he googled the market, his phone took him to downtown Cleveland, almost an hour away, where there was a similarly named store.

After arriving, Dad braved the crowded aisles and waited in line at the deli until the butcher was able to assist. The butcher found no record of a Pellegrino ham order. Dad dialed home.

"Lin, they don't have a ham under our name," he said, clearly at the end of his rope after driving so far for a ham.

Mom put Dad on speaker so her hands were free to prep her charcuterie board.

"What's taking you so long? It's six o'clock! My company will be here at eight!"

"It took me an hour to get here!"

"Mazzulo's is right down the street, Gar!"

"I'm in downtown Cleveland."

"What are you doin' in downtown Cleveland? My ham is at Mazzulo's!"

"I'm at Mazzulo's!"

As my dad's temper flared, I heard a voice in the background. "Sir, this is Constantino's."

He'd gone to the wrong place.

"Gary! I said Mazzulo's! Not Constantino's! Your father never listens—" Mom said to me while still on with Dad.

"Where's Mazzulo's?" he asked.

"You better hurry. They close at six, and it's already five after."

"If they closed five minutes ago and I'm an hour away, how do you expect me to get there on time?"

"I don't have time for math problems, Gar! Just get my ham!"

"Let me ask Constantino's if they have any fucking ham left."

The butcher was now helping someone else, so Dad waited impatiently while Mom sat on the edge of her seat, hoping they had a spare roast beast.

"Well, do they have any fucking ham, Gar?"

"Do you have any fucking ham here?" Dad asked the butcher at not-Mazzulo's, cutting the line by raising his voice in hope of an answer.

"Sir, it's not your turn," another customer shouted back.

"No, it's Christmas Eve. We're all out."

"Fuck," Dad replied, angrier than ever.

You know those tubes of crescent rolls that pop open? You slowly start to peel the paper off them, then twist and BAM! The dough comes oozing out so quickly. That's how my mom is on holidays. When tensions get so high, she pops. Almost every other year, she's the one losing it, the person threatening to cancel Christmas and leave the family high and dry, but when Dad is also losing it, Mom goes to the opposite end of the spectrum and instead does something that never fails to make my dad even angrier...she laughs at him. It's truly my favorite thing in the entire world. Dad is going nuts, swearing, stomping around like a child who needs a cigarette, his blood pressure at an all-time high, which is how he was that evening in the Italian market. When he gets like that, my mom starts to chuckle at him, unable to control her church giggles, spreading the joy to her sons, so then we all laugh at Dad, who's in the middle of a temper tantrum. The laughter makes him angrier, which makes

Mom laugh even harder. This time was no different: she struggled to catch her breath, endorphins flowing through her body for the first time all season, finally enjoying the sweet release of giggling at her husband's uncontrollable anger.

My boyfriend watches all those murder mystery shows and true crime docs about the wives who snap and kill their husbands, and talking heads try to figure out what happened in those last moments before a murder, and I always picture my parents fighting: Mom in a guttural laughing fit, tears flowing and her stomach hurting from crouching over when tensions are at their most high. If only one of those spouses who did the killing got the church giggles instead of murdering their significant other...

Alas, Mom still wanted her entrée, so she stopped her smiles momentarily to ask her hubby to stop somewhere else for the main dish.

"Gar, can you stop by the Giant Eagle? They're a bigger store, so they might have a ham. Now, it's Giant Eagle in Solon, Ohio, not Giant Eagle in Michigan. Don't drive to Michigan," she said, unable to get out the word *Michigan* without bursting back into laughter.

I stood beside her, holding my own stomach as I laughed my head off, knowing that my father has almost no patience and would surely not take Mom's joke in stride.

Silence.

"Gar, did you hear me? I don't want you goin' to the airport to fly somewhere else for a holiday ham—" she said, laughing harder than ever.

"Get your own fucking ham!" he said as he hung up.

We didn't have any roast pig that year, but we did laugh as we verbally roasted Dad. He got home an hour later, and as he entered the house, Mom attempted to apologize, but he couldn't make out the "sorry" over the howling. When she was finally able to curb the chuckling, she reached for his hand.

"Sorry we laughed. We thought you knew where Mazzulo's was."

As she finished her sentence, she remembered how far he drove and how all of it was for naught. It caused the laughter to return as she gently held his hand.

"We don't need any fucking ham," Dad said before heading into the basement and putting on the only thing that calms him down in a state of rage…a nature documentary.

Dad was right. Food is something that brings us all together, whether we're eating around a dinner table or laughing at our loved ones for driving an hour away to (not) get it. Eating it is great, but the best part is the tradition of gathering, cooking, or baking with the ones we love—and breaking bread while telling the story of Dad losing his temper at a faraway grocery chain because of the *fucking* holiday ham.

Just Like Santa Claus (Ho, Ho, Ho Remix)

Have you ever worked a seasonal job? I'm not talking about your year-round employment or everyday nine to five; I'm talking retail during the months of November and December, when people are at their most ghoulish and the loudspeaker is playing the same "Baby, It's Cold Outside" playlist over and over and over and over and over...

Seasonal employment is hellish but necessary when you must pay for gifts and decorations and baking supplies and ice-skating. The holidays are expensive! And I've always worked, but I need a little extra help come November, which is how I found myself in the setting for our next tale: Borders.

Sadly, this establishment no longer exists. We still have our beautiful Barnes & Nobles and indie bookstores, but back in the early 2000s, Borders bookstores were *everywhere*, including the suburban town of Solon, Ohio, where I grew up. The store opened during my teen years, and I was immediately obsessed. I'd beg my mom to take me or convince her she needed something at the Bed Bath & Beyond that was next door so I could go in and read mags and look at books. Because of *You've Got Mail,* I associated big-city living with booksellers and coffee, which is why having a Borders in my small town seemed like such a huge deal; it was the closest I could get to living my New York City dreams. Plus, they had gay stuff inside, so I could sneak the *Advocate* magazine and read about Danny from *The Real World* without anyone knowing.

I first applied to work there when I was in high school, but they weren't quite ready to hire me. That all changed my freshman year because my school was on a quarter system, unlike most of the other colleges in Ohio, which were on a semester schedule. OU students had an extra-long winter break, making us the perfect candidates for retail jobs over the holidays. I was officially on my way to my Nora Ephron fantasy as a Borders cashier (one of five-ish people manning the registers at any given moment).

I loved it. Even though the customers were nightmares and I was mostly just selling them all *Planet Earth* DVDs, I was living my best Meg Ryan life. Technically, I was working for more of the Tom Hanks storefront, but in my head, I was Meg with the cute short haircut and teacher skirts. There was something soothing about going into work and getting a custom coffee and being surrounded by cozy decor. Sure, there were downsides. I was/am a terrible gift wrapper, so anytime a customer asked me to wrap anything, they would inevitably be disappointed. Did you ever see that episode of *Saved by the Bell* when A.C. Slater gets a job wrapping at the mall? It's the same episode I mentioned earlier where Zack takes on the California homelessness crisis. Slater accidentally ties his finger to the bow he ties for Lisa. My wrapping was like that. (PS: Sorry for bringing up a 1991 Saturday-morning show starring Mark-Paul Gosselaar more than once in this book, but that's who I am.) I eventually started warning people, "I know I have to wrap if you ask me to, but I'm not good." Nicer customers would take their goods and tell me they would handle it themselves, some would wait for another employee to become available, and others would make me go through the motions of wrapping their junk and then swiftly unwrap before they got out of the store because I did such a bad job.

Detour

We must take a little detour here so I can tell you about the unfortunate time a kid pooped on the floor in front of the Dr. Seuss display. Literally, he just shit on the floor. I still don't quite understand how it happened. Not to mention hours went by until one of the employees noticed. There's so much going on at that time of year, and foot traffic in the store was at an all-time high. Nowadays, most people do their shopping online, but back then, the stores were loaded. It wasn't until the doors were closed that my coworker Teri announced on the loudspeaker, "Another kid pooped in the children's section." That's right, *another*. It had happened before.

I was still mid-gift wrap with a lingering customer when the announcement was made. "That's why I don't shop with my kids," the woman told me before exiting.

I then went to the back of the store to survey the damage. The store had special carpeting in the kid's section that looked like a solar system. I initially assumed it was meant to be whimsical, but turns out it was to camouflage child excrement. My manager told me the celestial design was great for covering up the occasional vomit and number twos until an employee could clean it up. No one knew exactly how long the poop had been there, but we do know multiple people had stepped in it. I don't remember this happening to Kathleen Kelly at the Shop Around the Corner, but I digress.

If there's one thing I learned from the *Facts of Life* theme song, it's that you take the good, you take the bad, and you take them both, and then you have the facts of life, so I never let the bad parts of the gig get me down, and I always knew the good outweighed those negatives. I remained positive, enjoyed living my dream, and sold a lot of books from November until January.

After the season ended, I was sad to go back to school. I missed my coworkers, the Lindor chocolate balls at the counter, and the free CDs they gave out in the employee break room. There was a whole bookcase filled with albums you could take home. They were returns, damages, and music that was played within the store, which is one of the few things I do *not* miss about the experience. When November hit, the store music became all Christmas, all the time. I love Céline Dion, she's a Canadian queen, but even a gay man will grow tired of her singing "O Holy Night" for eight hours a day. The store played *a lot* of Céline's *These Are Special Times*, an album that was released years earlier but still was played over and over and over and over—a balm for the Midwestern moms who frequented the establishment.

Sophomore year of college, I wrapped up my finals and headed home in early November, where I would once again work at Borders. When I arrived behind the cash register for year two, I heard Céline once again singing holiday hymns and, inexplicably, a ballad duet with R. Kelly (who appears on her holiday album).

By the eighth listen of the *Titanic* songstress's "Feliz Navidad," I snapped.

"Can we please listen to something else? Anything else?" I begged my manager.

"Customers buy a lot of copies of Céline," Teri (my manager) told me.

Teri was nice and always busy. She was a fiftysomething woman, which is my ideal demographic, and she ran a tight ship, working through breaks and only sharing personal info while she was stocking or doing something productive with her hands. I loved hearing about her marital struggles and hyping her ass up anytime she was down like the gay best friend in a '90s rom-com that I was born to be. Despite how much I love this demo, they cannot be relied on to choose music. No one other than young gay men should make public playlists. If you're not a young gay man, by all means, go listen to what you want on your headphones. But if you're in charge of store music or a workout class, you *must* hand the auxiliary cord over to a young gay man immediately.

"Can I put something else on? What if I make a new Christmas mix with other divas?" I asked.

As the words left my lips, I worried Teri would think I was gay.

"I don't know. Are there other diva Christmas songs?" she asked.

"Mariah, of course, Whitney Houston, and Cher..."

"What Christmas songs does Cher have?"

I panicked. Cher never did release a full holiday album. Aside from her work on the Sonny and Cher show, the only holiday song I could think of was the bop she'd done as a duet with Rosie on the Rosie O'Donnell Christmas album. They sang "Christmas (Baby Please Come Home)" together, recorded during the "Believe" era. I WAS NOT OUT. I couldn't mention Cher's song with Rosie as an example of her holiday musical output, could I?

I'm not a good liar, never was. I get caught up in the lie, adding too many other lies on top of the original lie, and I'm completely unable to keep everything straight. Here I was, trying to convince my manager I wasn't gay and that Cher had a holiday album. They were just two lies, but two too many for me.

"'Just Like Jesse James' by Cher is a Christmas song!" I lied.

For the unfamiliar, "Just Like Jesse James" *is* a Cher song, but it's not for trimming the tree. In fact, it's unlike almost any other song in her catalog, which is probably why I decided to use it for my cover-up. It's country-esque (or the most country Cher has ever gotten on a track). It was the most masc hit of hers I could think of in the moment.

"I don't even know that song. It's Christmassy?" Teri asked.

"Yes, I'll play it for you!" I said.

I mentioned earlier the back room had all sorts of CDs for the taking. They were open-box albums that they couldn't retail. Some people would take a CD home, burn it onto their computer, and put it back on the shelf. I grabbed *The Very Best of Cher* album and played it on the employee disc changer.

Teri was completely distracted, trying to schedule an entire store's worth of employees who didn't want to work on Christmas Eve. As she looked at her lists, I grabbed a nearby bell from one of the decorations. On my thigh, I shook the bell as the opening Cher chords came on the speaker, trying my best to not allow Teri to see the bell.

"Okay, whatever, you can play a holiday diva mix if you make sure it's all Christmas songs," she said before our "Turn Back Time" queen even got to the chorus.

That night, I went home with one goal: to become a music producer. I was familiar with burning CDs; I have countless albums from high school (most of which contain "Can't Fight the Moonlight" by LeAnn Rimes and at least twenty-seven that have Mandy Moore's "Only Hope" on them), but I wasn't just making a mixtape. I had to figure out a way to fashion a pop/country song into something that could appear alongside Brenda Lee. I needed a jingle bell.

Luckily, I was gifted a karaoke machine when I was younger, and my parents kept it in their basement since they never throw anything away. It came with a karaoke cassette with holiday music on it, so I downloaded Cher from Napster and somehow layered the song over the backing track of "Jingle Bells" from the karaoke tape. I know you're all reading my book right now, but I probably should've gone into audio engineering as a profession instead of writing.

The next day, I went into work with my new CD ready to go. The homemade album started off with classic Mariah singing about what she wants for Christmas, then a little Whitney belting "Do You Hear What I Hear?"* and in the middle, I had Cher's "Just Like Jesse James (Danny's Jingle Bell Mix)."

Teri took me to the disc changer set up to play throughout the store, so I loaded in the album and got in my spot behind the cash register. The music never plays too loud in those stores, but it was loud enough to hear while people browsed. I watched stressed-out customers checking items off their lists as the mix played. With bated breath, I waited for the Cher song to come on, anxious to see how people would react. Would they hum along? Would they be confused? Would

---

* Whitney's "Do You Hear What I Hear?" is important. Go listen to it immediately.

there be complaints that we were playing a song essentially about butt sex?

When Cher's silky voice kicked in and she started singing about giving it and taking it and something about a loaded gun, the customers looked happier than ever. The lyrics of the song are troubling, to say the least, and many gay people take the song to be a euphemism for anal. Even so, the stunning vocal delivery seemed to make everyone happy, everyone except Teri, who was looking confused as she restocked the children's shelves with copies of *The Polar Express*.

"What is this Cher song even about? What does Jesse James have to do with Christmas?" she asked.

"It's a Catholic thing," I said, knowing Teri was Jewish and admittedly not familiar with all the ins and outs of the Catholic holiday traditions. "Jesse James was originally one of the wise men. There were four, but he left the others and went into town. After Mary had Jesus, she went into town, and he tried to have sex with her. 'Cause she was a virgin."

"I will never understand your religion," she exclaimed, succumbing to the idea of Mary wanting to get fucked by Jesse James after the immaculate conception.

The song played four more times on my shift; each time filled me with glee as I watched the store patrons furrow their brows and wonder why this song was playing, why there was a jingle bell sound on the track, and how they'd missed the remix of such a classic Cher hit when it had been initially released. The song would end with a Santa voice saying, "Ho, ho, ho,

Merry Christmas," as it was part of the karaoke track I used, making it even more of a mindfuck.

Retail work is hard, especially during the holidays, so oftentimes sales associates have to make their own fun. Be nice to them while you do your shopping, and if you're a seasonal worker fed up with a playlist, remember: you can add a jingle bell to any song to make it Christmas music.

8-Bit Nostalgia

Tickle Me Elmo was the hot holiday toy of 1996. Originally developed as a Tickle Me Taz (based on the Looney Tunes property), the technology was better suited for *Sesame Street*'s toddler-friendly character. As legend has it, the toy was doing well enough, but an appearance on Rosie O'Donnell's daytime talk show sent its sales into the stratosphere, and the manufacturer couldn't keep up with demand. That same year, a movie called *Jingle All the Way* was released starring Arnold Schwarzenegger and Sinbad in which a dad tries to get a toy for his son on Christmas. There had been other moments in history when one toy dominated the industry at the end of the calendar year (Cabbage Patch Kids, Teddy Ruxpin, Furby, etc.), but its popularity seemed to reach a peak in that holiday season of 1996, crystalizing both in pop culture (the movies) and practice (store shelves) the notion that one toy will be an absolute must-have each year for the holidays. The one that meant the most to me was the Nintendo.

Detour

Lately, it feels like there's never any one toy that dominates, and I have my theories. Perhaps it's because we're all segregated into our own little bubbles of social media, so we don't have the same universal touchstones. Rosie reached everyone with her Elmo plug, and it felt authentic. In the world of influencer marketing, consumers are trained to be skeptical about what their favorite celebs are shilling and savvy enough to know the influencers are getting paid to hawk the products, but back in 1996, audiences knew Rosie was genuinely a fan.

Have you ever heard of Chiptune? It's the type of music in old video game consoles like the NES (short for Nintendo Entertainment System) or Game Boy. Remember when you would blow into a cartridge, stick it into the machine, and press START? The music that plays is called Chiptune. The sounds can still take me back to Christmas Day. As I'm sure you can tell by now, I'm wildly nostalgic for my youth, so I have quite an attachment to old-school video games. One year for Christmas, my older brothers asked for an NES, and my parents scraped enough money together to get them one. It was the hot holiday item and the only thing they wanted.

Christmas morning 1989, we got up at 5:00 a.m., opened our gifts, and rummaged through stockings filled with M&M's and Life Savers candies. I was happy with pretty much anything I got at that age.

"Mom, look what I got! I didn't even want it!" I happily shouted after opening socks.

After all the gifts under the tree had been accounted for, Mom coyly told us, "I think Santa might've left one more present in the garage." Parents always think they're tricking kids with that one. The kids know the game they're playing, but no one cares if it means another toy is on its way out. If you're reading this and you're a parent, just make sure that "one last present" is something fun and not socks.

Dad stood up amid the sea of discarded gift wrap and toy packaging and headed to the garage to grab a square box wrapped in reindeer paper. I wish I could insert the old home movie we have from that morning into this paragraph, but it's probably for the best that I can't because the shaky cam is worse than *The Blair Witch Project*. The tape also cuts between our old living room and an episode of *All My Children* because Mom used the VHS to record her stories.

To Bryan and Jr., From Santa, the tag said, in handwriting that was obviously my mom's, but she'd capitalized every letter to throw us off the scent. My brothers ripped it open, hoping it would be the NES they wanted so badly. Once the controller was visible through the tear above the top hat and button eyes, the screams followed.

Horror-movie scream queens wish they could reach the decibel and power of a child's yell when they open a video game system on a holiday. The energy in the room was electric. I was giddily playing with my *101 Dalmatians* stuffed animals when the vibe shift happened. The NES wasn't even something I knew about—I was four—but the happiness was contagious. It was like we all got a shot of espresso in our systems, dancing around the living room like that scene in *Titanic* when Leo and Kate lock arms and twirl. Mom and Dad were smiling from ear to ear.

Everything else took a back seat that day. Grandma and Grandpa would have to wait for their hugs, none of us cared about eating the lasagna and ham, and church was but a detour to getting in front of the TV where we could play *Super Mario Bros.*, the revolutionary new game that came packaged in the box. Since it wasn't technically a gift for me, I never got to hold the controller. Instead, I sat, legs crossed, and watched an 8-bit plumber jump from platform to platform, hopping on turtles and avoiding Bowser's fiery attacks. It was love at first sight.

The graphics were mind-blowing, but without being able to play, I focused on the music in those first few moments with the Nintendo. The "da-da-da-da-da-dada..." wiggled its way into my brain almost immediately. Come December 25, most of us are trying to get "Jingle Bells" out of our heads, and somehow *Super Mario* was able to do it almost instantly, before even reaching the underworld of the next level. In fact, the only melody that could replace the intro music was the sinister tune of level two.

I wonder how many families were humming those tunes on Christmas morning that year. Countless kids connected the AV cords to their big-ass TVs and played until nightfall or until their parents sent them to bed so they could have a turn.

Before then, many households had the Atari system, playing games like *Pong* and *Frogger*, but the NES was the first to come with an earworm. That Mario theme is one of the most recognizable tunes of all time, something people across the world know almost immediately from the opening notes.

I wonder what it must've been like for musicians to hear that music for the first time. How many young people listened to the Mario melody and realized a whole new world was available to them? Music majors and classically trained violinists suddenly had a new career path, one that allowed them to mix the technological advancements of the '80s with their love of music and traditional instruments. People who thought they wanted to be rock stars suddenly realized they could work in gaming, utilizing their music skills in a different way.

Koji Kondo is the brilliant mind behind that *Super Mario Bros.* theme, and he's created some of the most memorable music in gaming ever since—like the NES *Zelda* theme, a haunting refrain that is just as beautiful as anything Beethoven ever composed.

Since that Christmas morning, I've heard the Mario music countless times. It's reprised in other video games, and it's also known to pop in my head at random when I'm grocery shopping or in the shower. When I like something, I tend to obsess, and there have been many sleepless nights I've spent on YouTube watching orchestral arrangements of video game themes from my youth. Eventually, I got my own turn with the controller, and when the Super Nintendo was released in 1991, I was ready for it. I was old enough to understand the mechanics, and Mario had become a friend to me like he became a friend to so many throughout the years. He's there for the children who aren't invited to the sleepovers, and he's there for you when your parents are fighting in the other room, when the sounds of their voices are too much to handle. Before I knew what anxiety was, Mario, Luigi, Toad, and Princess Peach were there to help me deal.

Mario has been with us for so many holidays. In 1996, he showed up for the first time in 3D on the N64. In 2001, his brother, Luigi, took center stage for the launch of the GameCube. In 2012, he was there for a lucky few who managed to get their hands on the Wii for Christmas. And most recently, he came to me via UPS in the dark days of 2020, the first year I spent Christmas without my immediate family as COVID-19 kept us all apart. I cried and cried and cried for days leading up to that sad December 25, but the tears subsided when I opened a gift from Mom and Dad, a new Switch game starring my favorite man in red overalls.

And that's the power these gifts hold. Gift giving may get harder as we all get older and find ourselves shopping for adults who have their own money to buy the things they want, but the experience of giving presents to kids is still just as fun and magical as it's always been. When you give a gift to a child, you get to open their imagination, show them things they couldn't see before, and give them a momentary reprieve from whatever they're struggling with. Video game systems are expensive, and many people can't afford to drop that kind of money on a gift for their kid, but children have imaginations that need encouragement. Whether it's a brand-new NES or a box of crayons and a ream of construction paper, a gift that sparks creativity can be a lifesaver for young people who need help expressing how they feel or piecing together the emotions bottled up inside them.

There's a scene in *Mrs. Doubtfire* where Robin Williams as Daniel Hillard, dressed as Euphegenia Doubtfire, is at a public pool with his family, watching a blouseless Pierce Brosnan splash around with his three kids and ex-wife. All the while, Robin sits at the bar in prosthetics and a dress under the hot San Francisco sun. It's a low point in the film for the character, but he powers through because he realizes the only thing that means anything in life is the time we spend with our loved ones. Daniel Hillard is living his personal hell, but his hell is worth it for more time with the people he loves most.

Parents feel pressure to make the holidays perfect for their kids, to get every item on their wish list, the must-have toys of the season, to bake the best cookies, and to honor the yearly traditions. They work extra shifts, participate in layaway plans, and go to six different stores trying to get the best gift. It's expensive and exhausting. If you're reading this and finding you're in the middle of the madness, stressed to the max and wondering how you're going to make it to the other side of December, take a moment instead to recalibrate. Sure, your child may have a smile on their face as they open a new bike or a laptop computer. They'll brag to their friends and spend the day playing with their shiny stuff. But the item isn't as important as the feeling of love you create just by being with them.

The best part is the smiling, the playing together. That's because the greatest gift you can give your children, or anyone for that matter, is your love. No one else can love like you can, so take the pressure off yourself and your wallet when it comes to the presents. If you have the funds to get the fancy toy and want to do it, go for it, but know that what is going to stick with your child in the end is the feeling of being loved and belonging to a family. When they're eighty and looking back on their lives, they'll remember being with you on the holiday. Be proud if you have a household filled with the love and togetherness that makes a home. Life is fleeting, so forget the rest. I give you permission.

Whenever I hear that old *Super Mario* music, I think about Christmas morning, surrounded by my loved ones in our tiny family unit. It's a unit that expanded so much since then, with wives and partners, nieces and nephews coming into the picture. We've also lost loved ones, grandparents and cousins and a few exes along the way, each shift altering the dynamics. Those special gifts—the ones parents work extra hard to get—will always be a link to the memory of life. Years from now, they'll be the thing that helps you trace back your todays to your yesterdays, so try and remember that as you're shopping for your little ones. Even if you can't put the fancy toy under the tree, the important thing is the feeling they have, so wrap them in your love, and know that even the most special presents are not as important as how you make them feel.

Detour

My nostalgia-heavy point of view can be exhausting; I get that. The writing in this book is dangerously close to Clint Eastwood yelling, "Get off my lawn," in the movie *Gran Torino*, but it's also my sweet spot. Helps me escape the present. And speaking of presents, one of my favorite holiday gifts growing up was the classic sitcom Christmas episode. In the '80s and '90s, TV shows produced around twenty-five episodes per season. The rise of streaming means we get technically brilliant shows that wrap up their entire storylines in four to six episodes, but we get less batshit insane programming due to writers not having to come up with so many storylines to fill the schedule. Everything is very nuanced now, but the broad sitcom days of yore were a beautiful time. The superlong seasons meant we got episodes for each holiday. *Roseanne* had must-watch Halloween shows, *Friends* owned Thanksgiving, and *Home Improvement* gave us Tim Allen yelling his signature "HUH!?" grunt as he was tangled in twinkle lights every December. I've already waxed poetic about *Full House* and *Saved by the Bell* throughout this book. I could write individual essays on each of these programs, but instead I want to highlight an oft-forgotten show starring a wisecracking alien from Melmac. *Alf* ran from 1986 to 1990, popping up in lots of other programming after that, but his second-season Christmas episode is something you all must see at least once in your lifetime—but do so with caution because it is a DOOZY. Seriously, no other holiday content is as depressing as the Alf special. You might think you remember the hilarious character making jokes and taking jabs at the Tanner family and laughing about eating cats, but in season two, he visits a children's hospital, faces mortality as he connects with a dying girl, then delivers a baby in an elevator. Oh, and Alf *also* stops a suicide when one of the hospital volunteers wants to end his life. You might think I'm being facetious or exaggerating, but it's all true. THIS HAPPENS IN AN ALF TWO-PARTER THAT AIRED ON NBC. A character literally starts to jump off a bridge, and Alf foils his plan while wearing a Santa suit. I like to imagine parents gathering their young kids around the televisions in 1987 to watch their favorite fuzzy puppet deliver some zings in front of a tree and instead had to explain life and death. At one point, the character of Alf literally has a tear in his eye, which means someone on the production team had to halt the scene where he connected with the ailing child to put some liquid on the puppet. He wasn't the only one crying because it's impossible to watch this two-parter without crying at home. It's haunting!

"Well, that sure was a lot," many '80s dads must have said as they wiped tears from their eyes and sent their kids off to bed before turning on *Perfect Strangers*.

We all need a release from the emotions we keep bottled inside, so let *Alf* be that release. Put on the *Alf* Christmas special, and let the tears flow.

New Year

The cardboard top hats are folded, wine-stained glitter sits at the bottom of an empty glass, and the faint echo of a Party City noisemaker fills the air. New Year's morning. Gross.

I know some people like to start fresh once the confetti is cleaned up on January 1, but I've never quite been able to embrace the big day or the night before. The closest I've come is seeing the movie *New Year's Eve,* a Garry Marshall film starring a million celebrities, in theaters. My friend Michael and I hooted and hollered during the extensive credits. People like Alyssa Milano, who showed up on screen for a quick thirty-second cameo, would normally be considered extras but were somehow spotlighted as movie stars since the entire appeal of these kinds of movies is that each speaking part is filled with a "star." The marketing machine behind the film wanted the audience to be blown away by the fact that they got Michelle Pfeiffer *and* Ludacris, even though they were barely on-screen. It's an insane film, and I love it.

My other problem with this holiday is that there's always so much pressure to have a good time. Forced fun is never fun. Bars are always too crowded, rideshares too scarce, restaurants too full and pricey, and if you're single, you're either pitied at midnight for not having someone to kiss, or you're face deep in some gay with hot dragon breath who your friend Kaitlyn thought you would get along with simply because you're both gay. Somehow, you wake up next to him naked with a sore jaw. Or so I've heard. I wish we could just ignore the day like I ignore birthdays.

The pressure for the perfect date also leads our pickers astray. We get drunk and text old lovers, strategically place ourselves at parties where we know we'll see an old flame, and even try to make it work with significant others who have long passed their expiration date.

I blame Y2K. NYE was always a pressured holiday, but the impending doom of the year 2000 heightened our emotions to unthinkable levels that never fully came down. I write this as a reminder to allow midnight to strike without the weight of the world on my shoulders. Perhaps it's enough to enter a new year with the calm surrender that you are enough. Sure, it's great to have someone beside you with mascara smudged on their new sweater or a job that you can't wait to get back to in a few days' time, but maybe just being you wherever you are is enough next year. And instead of making resolutions we won't keep, simply take stock of the good you've already accumulated. Enjoy the ding of a sloppy text from a parent or long-distance friend…or ex. Whatever you have is enough. It's a blessing to enter another cycle, so happy New Year.

"Auld Lang Syne" is a New Year's classic, and the song starts with "Should old acquaintance be forgot and never brought to mind?" It's a reminder to cherish the memories, honor the past, and take stock of your life before the future starts.

PS: Don't forget to stock up on ibuprofen for the hangover (and lockjaw).

Shakespeare, We're in Love (At Christmastime)

No holiday collection would be complete without a twinkle-light rom-com, like the kind that inhabits the airwaves from October to January (and pops up most Fridays on the Hallmark channel). We all know the movies I'm talking about—big-city gal goes back to her hometown before Christmas, falls in love with the hunky townie from high school, and climaxes in a single kiss as they go for a stroll after the town tree lighting. The male lead is usually exceptional at just one thing: running an inn, construction, app development—hell, I've even seen one where the guy was an expert at bird-watching. There's never any sex and rarely any gay people, but the holiday season fills every inch of the television screen as the beats play out. It's magical, predictable, like visual Xanax.

Each one is almost exactly the same, and yet every year, there are more and more of them. Some people loathe them, while others like me tune in to each one the machine wants to feed us. Sometimes I'm not even sure if I'm watching one

I've seen already or if the familiarity of Lacey Chabert building a gingerbread house is warping my brain waves. Watching feels like a warm, familiar hug from an old friend. You know you're settling in for a few hours of Christmas cheer, with no real-world craziness seeping in. It's barely even evident what year the films are made because they're meant to be evergreen. Watching a Hallmark or Lifetime holiday movie from 2003 is essentially the same experience as watching one from 2023.

Despite the fondness I have for these made-for-TV movies, I can recognize the shortcomings. Although there is considerably more diversity in the cast of characters on-screen nowadays, they're not exactly known for the gay representation. I can count on my hands how many of the literal hundreds of original movies from the past two decades feature LGBTQ+ characters, let alone LGBTQ+ lead characters (fortunately, it *is* getting better every year). Since there are so few people highlighting my big gay experience, I thought I would do it here in this book. If you don't see something, write something... That's the saying, right? Maybe I'm getting my wires crossed, but I'm here and I'm queer, and I'm ready to sweep you off your cynical feet with my own twinkle-light romance!

Fortunately, I don't have to work too hard to come up with a plot. One of my first (gay) relationships was a twinkle-light romance. Big-city gay falls for small-town homosexual over the holiday season! Technically, we were both in the same city, and the other gentleman was not a hunky construction worker and instead a trained (still hunky) Shakespearean actor, but the beats are (mostly) the same...ish. Now on to our meet-cute!

My first winter living in Chicago proper was tough. Coming from Ohio suburbia, I had left my network of friends behind to make it in a big city, but I wasn't quite prepared for the extreme weather (Illinois is much windier than Cleveland). I worked my ass off, taking on any job I could to pay my ridiculously high rent and waking up when it was still dark out so I could catch the train to the office where I temped. The cold winds as I waited for the red line were brutal at 6:00 a.m. It didn't matter how many pairs of long underwear or gloves I wore, waiting for the train sent my body into shock. So much shock that I had a bout of pneumonia that left me briefly hospitalized in month two.

When I finally recovered in late November, I was ready to move onward and upward, determined to leave the bad luck behind me and adjust to my new city. I invested in another layer of long johns and settled into work as a temp at a real estate office. In hopes of being hired full-time after my temp contract ended, I agreed to overtime and volunteered to run extra errands for my boss, the evil Mr. Tiskman, a man who reveled in bulldozing trees for large industrial complexes, a man who survived on energy drinks and extramarital affairs.

"Danny, you're into artsy stuff, right?" Mr. Tiskman asked

one afternoon when he overheard me listening to the *Wicked* soundtrack at my desk.

"I take some improv classes downtown on the weekends, but—"

"Great, my daughter's school is looking for a director for her Christmas play. The person they had was caught with booze at the rehearsal."

There was no question mark attached to his statement, so I was slightly confused when he seemed to suggest I was destined to take charge of this school play without much incentive. Powerful men like Mr. Tiskman have a delusional self-confidence, which always works in their favor. It was a delusion I envied as the meek and cowering closeted twenty-two-year-old I was, trying to survive in a big city that favored grit.

"Are you asking me to...?"

"Take over the school play, yeah. My wife is driving me crazy about it. I can't hear about it anymore, so please, just do the last couple of rehearsals, and I'll pay you hourly under the table."

"I'm not, like, a theater expert. I'm still in level-one improv, and I barely have any free time. I'm still living out of my suitcase after four months!"

"You'll be fine. I know you listen to that Broadway crap, and the kids are all twelve and under."

"*Wicked* is not crap, it's—"

"My wife will email you details," he said.

Before I could launch into my explanation of why "Defying Gravity" is one of the greatest American songs of all time, Mr.

Tiskman was gone. And days later, I was walking into a private school gymnasium and meeting with Mr. Tiskman's wife, who introduced me to twelve kids under the age of twelve, all of whom were sugared up from the red velvet cupcakes that the previous director had sent as an apology for no longer being able to work with them due to his drinking problem.

The first rehearsal was a complete blur. The students were doing a *Gift of the Magi*-esque story about a daughter selling her bicycle to buy her dad a hammer and the dad selling his hammer to buy a bike seat for his daughter. Some of the young children were playing grown adults, while others were children. They claimed to have a script memorized, but no one had a copy of said script, so I had no idea if they were actually reciting the correct lines (and every young mind had a differing opinion about what the dialogue was). I spent most of that rehearsal staring in awe at the chaos around me. I imagine this was how Ryan Murphy felt on the set of *Glee*.

As the kids were picked up by the parents two hours later, I made plans to visit a bar to unwind. I understood why the previous guy was liquored up all the time; these children were *exhausting*. Although I didn't have many friends in the city, that wasn't going to stop me from getting the drink I'd earned. While seated solo at my favorite watering hole, a place in the middle of a holiday karaoke night, I spotted a cute guy, also by himself, reading. With a Shakespeare play in one hand and pen in the other, he was making notes as he scanned the pages, sipping his hot toddy topped with whipped cream in between underlining.

Shockingly, he was able to concentrate as a smattering of out-of-tune homosexuals sang Judy Garland, but alas, he was in the zone, never once looking up to see who was rocking around the Christmas tree. Normally, I would've ignored him, spent time on my phone scrolling through Twitter, but something took hold of me. Perhaps it was some reverberating chutzpah from the beautiful trans woman who was singing "Last Christmas" on key.

"I though the point of a bar is that you go when you're done working?" I shouted from a few seats over.

"Work is pleasure for me," he replied, finally looking up from his book.

"Shakespeare is pleasure?"

"If you do it right."

I took a sip of my vodka soda and moved closer to the mystery man who looked like a budget, less-super-but-still-gorgeous Henry Cavill, a ballsy move I chalked up to my last vodka soda. The man put his book down and confidently looked into my eyes.

"I'm Jesse."

A beat went by before I realized he wasn't going to ask my name, a power move to match my moving seats.

"I'm Danny. Nice to meet you. I never could get into Shakespeare, too hard to understand."

"I'm an actor, so—"

"No way! I'm an actor too!" I bragged.

At this point, I never anticipated this man to be more

than a possible make-out before bed. My audacious flirting aside, I had never done more than hook up with a guy. I certainly never entertained the idea of a relationship. Flirting was always a means to an end that included sex without the romance and then never speaking again unless it was to kiss after a night of drinking.

"You're an actor, but you don't know Shakespeare? It's the foundation of acting!"

"You're one of *those* actors—"

"What kind of actor are you?" he asked.

"Well, I'm teaching right now. Technically, I'm directing a play," I replied, giving myself entirely too much credit. Jesse didn't need to know I was barely in charge, my students were under twelve, and I was less hired and more forced by someone who was (sort of) my boss. I was the production babysitter.

"If you're teaching, you *must* know Shakespeare. I know of a class you could take—"

"I'm so busy right now. I wish I had time for a class," I said.

"You're at a bar, alone, at eight o'clock on a Tuesday, and you're young. You don't have time?"

"I mean, technically my nights are free, but I'm—"

"Good. I know of a class, one night a week, seven thirty to ten."

"No, I, uh, I mean—" I was too slow to find a way out, so I was thrilled when he changed the subject.

"You going to sing tonight, kid?"

Kid? He was barely thirty, a handful of years older than I was.

"No, no, I don't sing. That's my gift to society: not singing."

"So you don't do Shakespeare, you don't sing, and you *still* consider yourself an entertainer?" he asked.

"When you say it like that, I mean, uh, um, I want to be—"

"I suppose those who can't do teach," he said with a smirk.

"It's not like I'm scared of those things. I just—"

"Sure, whatever. Obviously you're scared."

"I'm not scared!" I asserted, raising my voice to levels I never had before.

"You're scared. Everyone can sing a little. You're just scared to."

I was determined to prove this man wrong out of spite. How dare he call me scared! I stormed up to the stage, a small platform covered in tinsel and garland, whispered into the ear of the older gentleman in drag running the amateur singing hour, and prepared to blow everyone away with my out-of-tune singing. The opening chords of the melancholy "Miss You Most (At Christmastime)" by Christmas queen Mariah Carey began to play. After just a few seconds, it was evident that my voice was less 1994 Mariah and more dying cat. The worse I got, the more the people cheered. I felt like Cameron Diaz in *My Best Friend's Wedding*, getting happier and happier the worse I got. The boos mixed with cheers as I wrapped up the holiday ballad with a smile. When I looked over at Jesse, I noticed he was smiling too, shocked at just how terrible I was at singing and somehow charmed by my tonelessness.

"I told you I wasn't scared."

"See what happens when you get out of your comfort zone?"

Even though I'd come out on top, he'd somehow manipulated the act into a win for him. It was impressive and would've been more so if he didn't have whipped cream on his nose from his hot drink.

"Looks like you're the one who's a little too comfortable," I said, pointing to his gorgeous nose.

"Excuse me?"

"You have whipped cream on your nose."

Rather than wipe it off, Jesse smeared it around his cheeks. His confidence was as contagious as it was infuriating, and it was enough to convince me to show up to this Shakespeare class he raved about.

"You really don't embarrass easily, do you?" I asked.

"Life is embarrassing. Might as well lean in."

"So where is this stupid Shakespeare class you were raving about?"

"Here," Jesse replied, grabbing my arm in the process and writing a phone number on my skin with his pen. "Call Susannah Kline. She'll save a spot for you. First week is free. And don't call it stupid ever again."

"Will do, old man," I said, matching his energy.

Jesse stood and began to put his coat and scarf on.

"Leaving already? What about your number—" I couldn't believe the words were leaving my mouth. I had never asked for a number before!

"I'll see you around," he replied, keeping his digits closer to the chest than I would have liked. He took the candy cane garnish off his empty hot toddy and started to make his way to the door.

"Wait! You still have whipped cre...never mind."

Jesse walked back up to my chair, reached across my chest for a cocktail napkin, so close that I could smell his peppermint breath. He wiped his nose inches away from my own face; I could see the creases in his lips, the stubble on his chin.

"Did I get it all?" he asked, looking deep into my soul with his stunning hazel eyes.

My heart was racing, wondering if our lips would meet for a kiss.

"You got it all," I said as he moved away from the moment.

"I'll see ya, kid."

Jesse's presence left me with a hangover. He was infuriating and intoxicating at the same time. I HATED this man but also fell madly in love.

Less than a week later, I showed up to the first Shakespeare class at the home of Susannah Kline, a woman who looked exactly like she taught drama classes out of her home. The Charlie Brown Christmas tree she had near the window obviously had been up all year, but she'd decided to finally turn on the lights after Thanksgiving. A handful of twenty- and thirty-somethings gathered in her living room. Kelly, a young woman I knew from the building where I worked, sat next to me.

"Hi! Omigod, you work on Monroe, right? I think you're in—"

"Yeah, I thought you look familiar. I see you at the commissary sometimes. I'm Danny."

"Kelly. Nice to meet you! I'm an actor. I mean, I work as an assistant, but it's only to pay for classes like this. Susannah is the best!"

"I'm not really into Shakespeare, but I met a guy who recommended it," I said.

"You don't understand—she is *the* best. People come from all over the country to work with her."

"For Shakespeare?"

"Yes! No one better in the country."

"Hm. Cool, I guess." I shrugged.

Other people filed in, each seemingly more excited than the last to be here. I started to get a contact high from all their iambic pentameter buzz.

"Omigod, omigod, omigod!" Kelly said as her cheeks turned red.

"What? What's wrong?" I asked.

"I can't believe he's here!"

"Who? Who's here?"

"He plays Edward the Third! I just saw his play last night at the Chicago Shakespeare Company!"

I looked up and there he was...

"It's Jesse Mendelson!" Kelly exclaimed. The rest of the room gasped as Jesse made his way to Susannah and gave her a big hug. The energy completely shifted; the crowd treated him like royalty.

I was horrified. Just the other night, I was bragging about being an actor and an acting teacher, all to a man who was seemingly one of the greatest living Shakespeare performers.

"Jesse is one of the greatest living Shakespeare performers!" Kelly confirmed.

"Everyone sit, everyone sit! We need to get started! We have a new student joining us, but *more importantly,* I'm sure you all know Jesse Mendelson. He's in town from New York, taking a hiatus from his hit Broadway shows to do Edward III at the Chicago Shakespeare Company, and he agreed to come by to show us a few things," Susannah said to the room.

"Hi! So nice to meet you all. Susannah taught me back when I lived here, and I always try to make it to her classes when I'm in town. This work is my passion, and I look forward to spending the next couple of hours showing you all why."

Everyone looked at Jesse as if he were Julia Roberts showing up at a Walgreens. Part of me wanted to run out the door and never look back; the other part of me wanted to stand up and brag about knowing Mr. Popular. Before I could decide—

"Danny! You made it. Good to see you!" Jesse said with a wink in front of the entire group.

I melted like a snowman in June. His cockiness was softened, and I was intoxicated by his influence. I was famous by association.

"Omigod, you know Jesse?" Kelly whispered.

"Kinda, sorta, maybe," I said.

The next two and a half hours were just as much of a blur as my first play rehearsal with the kids; I spent the entire time trying to figure out if I should stay behind to talk to Jesse or sprint out of that drama house as soon as the clock struck ten.

The choice was made for me when Susannah wrapped up class by calling for me to stay behind. Something about payment and logistics, since I was joining a group that had already had a week together.

Kelly and most of the others slowly filtered out of the home, and I sat idle while Susannah chatted with one last student who needed some help with his *Othello* monologue. Jesse ran to the restroom and came back to sit in the empty chair next to me with an annoying grin he had from so many people kissing his ass all night.

"You learn something, kid?"

"Ya know, I don't think I'm that much younger than you."

"You sure do act like you're younger," he countered.

"How dare you? You're the immature one who didn't even tell me you were some big Shakespeare guy."

We playfully argued like Sandra Bullock and whatever male lead she is starring alongside until Susannah was ready to chat about payment. I hated him even more than I had at the bar, and yet I desperately wanted him to like me. It was pathetic. *I* was pathetic, but the heart wants what it wants, and mine wanted to prove I could win over this jerk who was also impressive and kind underneath his frustrating (and gorgeous) exterior. My proximity to Jesse got me a friends-and-family discount, so I was able to spend the next three weeks in December learning about Hamlet and company in between kid rehearsals and busy office work during the day. I loved it, even though I was also completely exhausted from all the personal growth I was doing.

Jesse invited me to attend the opening night of *Edward III* in early December. He offered me two tickets, the best in the house, and Kelly tagged along. He was brilliant; I was so mad. Up until the play, I'd thought maybe he was just okay, that maybe the people raving about his work hadn't actually seen him perform. Unfortunately, even I could tell he was great. Seeing him onstage was breathtaking. One show turned me into a Shakespeare junkie; I couldn't get enough. I got to work memorizing a monologue for class, and I even did some fancy acting exercises I learned with the kids as a rehearsal warm-up. Seeing eleven-year-olds do a piece from *The Tempest* was tough, but I became obsessed with the deceased playwright. There was a child who was originally supposed to play a shop owner in the school play, and I turned his dialogue into iambic pentameter (which ended up sounding more like *One Fish, Two Fish, Red Fish, Blue Fish*).

The whole time I got to know Jesse (and Bill Shakespeare), I was still closeted. No one in my life knew I was gay. I snuck out to queer bars in the city alone, and I didn't personally know many folks in the city outside the crowd I was getting to know at work and my extracurriculars. The people closest to me were back in Ohio, and my fear of coming out kept a wall up when I met others, preventing me from getting too close. That all changed, and Kelly was the first person I officially came out to, and it was largely because of my crush on Jesse. She was so impressed that I knew him, it was easy to let her know it was potentially romantic. I was empowered by it.

After Jesse's premiere, he asked me on an actual date-date, and I panicked. Flirting at a bar or after an acting class was one thing, but a real date seemed dangerous! Jesse was so comfortable in his skin, and I realized that had rubbed off on me. It's why I had managed to get onstage and sing Mariah in front of strangers at holiday karaoke, it's how I found out I had a love of Shakespeare, and it's why I said yes to a night out on the town with a man who was moving back to New York after the holiday season.

Jesse told me that the theater production put him up in a hotel downtown, and he wanted to know if I would come and have dinner with him. Our date night rolled around. I put on my finest wares and took public transportation to the hotel. He met me downstairs, and we had a nice dinner nearby at a quiet pub—the kind of place that only Chicago does right. After our plates were cleared, Jesse grabbed my hand to hold it. My whole body tensed, worried about what would happen when our waiter saw me holding the hand of another man. Before finding out, I yanked my fingers away from him and put my hands under the table. How was Jesse so comfortable being himself in public? Not just himself but *romantic*! With another man! It was astounding to me.

We finished our cocktails pretty late, and Jesse asked if I wanted to go for a walk around the city. He knew of some cool areas I'd never been that he wanted to show me. We walked around well after midnight and began to explore the streets that were covered in snow from earlier in the week. In urban areas like Chicago, people are always out and about; nothing ever quiets down too much. As we walked through the beautiful downtown, he grabbed my hand again. *He grabbed my hand again!* Like, he held my hand. In public! We weren't even surrounded by walls in a dimly lit restaurant. Not only that, but I also held it back this time, and I felt happy inside!

The night turned out to be the first real date I'd ever had. Those evenings in high school and college with girls I pretended to have a crush on were nothing like this; this was what romance was supposed to feel like. It was butterflies and exhilaration. We walked hand in hand under the city sky, his skin keeping me warm. We stopped on a bridge overlooking the river that was lined with twinkle lights, and it began to snow.

"Isn't the snow magical? The way it covers all the dirt and grime on the streets, making everything look fresh and new," Jesse said as he looked out over the frozen water.

The moment was too special for me to reply verbally; instead, I surprised even myself by grabbing Jesse's red flannel shirt, pulling him close, and kissing him as snowflakes fell, melting as they seeped between our lips. A group of carolers walked by, singing and jingling some gold bells, but I wasn't scared at all. The fear of someone finding out my little gay secret was nothing compared to the thrill of falling in love for the first time.

We had two more amazing weeks together. Jesse came by the school play I directed; he coached me on my *Measure for Measure* monologue for Susannah's class.

"Thus stands it with me! Upon a true contract..."

"No, no, no! There's a rhythm!" he said frustratingly from

the comforts of a luxurious penthouse suite bed that his producers paid for.

Jesse had to go back to New York, and I arranged to spend Christmas with my family back in Ohio. We made plans to see each other in the new year, me visiting NYC and him letting me know when he could make it to the Windy City, but the truth is life isn't always like a picture-perfect Hallmark movie. If it were, the credits would've rolled after our first big-city kiss. We never saw each other again. Our relationship wasn't meant to last, but he was still one of my great loves because he taught me to love myself. He showed me bravery and romance, confidence, and the beauty of a first kiss in the snow.

My love of Shakespeare and the written word continued; plus, I got the full-time contract at the real estate office thanks to the school play going off without a hitch. There were other men ahead for me in the city too: a cowboy, a pilot, and a bartender. I only stayed at the job for a little while before moving to another state myself, something I heard Mr. Tiskman's wife did too, with a man named Robert (Kelly would update me every few months about all the drama back in Chicago).

A handful of years after my time with Jesse, I was dating someone new, the guy I'm with now, a man I would've never met if I hadn't spent that winter with Jesse getting comfortable in my own skin. I decided, like William S., I would write my own little sonnet to my lost love Jesse in the form of an email. It wasn't quite as poetic as *Romeo and Juliet* or *Othello,* but it was from the heart...

J,

I've been meaning to write you for a while, to thank you. I know we barely got to know each other, but you came into my life at a time when I needed it most. I didn't think I would be able to fully come out. I struggled for years to be myself, and I was instantly attracted to your confidence because I had none. You seemed so sure of yourself, and I had never known a gay person so comfortable in their own skin. Aside from the amazing example you set, you introduced me to Susannah and the language of Shakespeare. My eyes were opened to so many new things. Even though I quickly understood that we wouldn't be more than friends, I'm grateful for the few nights when I was in a world I had never been. There was a moment when you grabbed my hand when we were walking down the street, a moment I'll never forget. Your company was great, but more importantly, I realized I could be myself in a world I thought was telling me to be someone else. You did more for me than people I have known my entire life, and for that I thank you. My instinct is to apologize for this hokey message, but instead I'll try and live in my bravery. I wish you the best of luck and hope for only great things in your future.

"Hear my soul speak. Of the very instant that I saw you, Did my heart fly at your service."—*The Tempest*, Act 3, Scene 1

With respect and love,

Danny

That was the end of our love story, a love story that laid the foundation for the romance I was meant for, and it showed me that the heart can fly.

Traditions

Sometimes we get caught up in ritual, thinking something we do one year for the holidays has to happen every year. There are religious celebrations and cultural events I don't take part in but respect tremendously. There are also those little things that certain families participate in that were never present in my life. Nowadays, kids do the Elf on the Shelf thing, but that wasn't something I participated in as a child (although I did buy my own Elf on the Shelf as an adult and put a cozy robe on him before taking pics of him in compromising positions for laughs).

One of my favorite traditions is with one of my best friends, Jill. We like to forgo gifts and instead spend the money going to cheap photo studios and taking dramatic professional pics with a confused photographer. The studios are usually set up for children, so we're often posing with absurd backdrops and insane props. We spend the whole time laughing. Here are some of my faves...

Here we are dramatically wrapped in a giant rosary. It's amazing I didn't burst into flames on the spot.

She was framed! For some reason they had an empty picture frame as a prop. Unclear why.

The photographer for this setup was incredibly confused.

Unfortunately, the publisher would not let me use this as the book cover.

I went through a "googly eye era" after purchasing these giant googly eyes. You can put them on everything to make it funny. Vaccuum cleaners, refrigerators, or your bestie.

This last one is a picture of us opening the gift of *Magic Mike* on Blu-ray, an item more valuable than gold, frankincense, or myrrh.

I get especially obsessed with pop culture customs and the way certain pieces of art are annually celebrated. As a talk show junkie, I *need* to see Darlene Love on the boob tube every December. She's a queen who has performed "Christmas (Baby Please Come Home)" year after year on *Letterman* and later revived it for *The View* when Dave was off the air. As much as I worship Darlene, I always imagine that if I had my own talk show, I'd invite Willa Ford on to sing her take on "Santa Baby" that appeared on an early 2000s CD called *MTV: A TRL Christmas*. I've had the same truck since 2006, a vehicle with a six-disc changer, one loaded with the *TRL* album, Mariah, Kelly, Jessica, and both Rosie O'Donnell Christmas albums come November. If I'm being honest, most of those are in there year-round.

TV networks are always programming old classics like *A*

Charlie Brown Christmas and *Rudolph the Red-Nosed Reindeer*. I've been terrified of those Claymation specials ever since I was a kid—something about the noise his nose makes leaves me uneasy—but it's impossible to miss it because it airs every year. *A Christmas Story* usually gets twenty-four-hour coverage on TBS. They filmed it near my hometown, and the owners offer yearly tours of the house so people can put on a pink bunny suit and walk around inside.

I like to read, so *Skipping Christmas* by John Grisham (which was later made into the film *Christmas with the Kranks*, a bonkers Tim Allen/Jamie Lee Curtis movie that is both five stars and also just one star) is read by the fire each December. A lot of parents read *The Polar Express* by Chris Van Allsburg to their kids during the holidays, and it's such a beautiful book that I often find myself lost in the pages when I see it at my nieces and nephews' houses. It was also made into a feature film using complex animation that wasn't quite ready to be used on humans. Here's a still frame from the movie...

Just kidding. That's actually a drawing my four-year-old nephew Brady drew for me, but it's more appealing to me than the creepy way they animated *The Polar Express*, even with the balls Brady inexplicably drew on the snowman. I've always been disappointed that there aren't more Christmas books for adults to enjoy yearly, which is why you're all getting this one. My dream is that people will pull *The Jolliest Bunch* out with their decorations and escape into the pages when the snow starts to fall. I hope these words will start to feel familiar and each chapter will feel like a warm blanket on a cold night.

One of the traditions I hold most dear is that of Oprah's Favorite Things list. This started as a special episode of her daytime talk show, and I remember rushing home from school, finishing my homework as quickly as possible, and then sitting down at 5:00 p.m. to watch. Oprah would gather an unsuspecting audience who thought they were there for a typical show. They'd be thrilled to hear wise words from Iyanla or watch Nate Berkus make over Jerry O'Connell's bachelor pad, but getting to be in the audience for a Favorite Things episode? Forget it. For the youths out there who never got a chance to witness this: Please, you must do your research and immediately go find one of them online. People died!* The best was 2010 when Ms. Winfrey stood in front of the crowd wearing a black dress and started blabbering on about meditation and how important it was.

---

* No one technically died, but I needed to be dramatic so you knew I was serious.

"How about we meditate on this?" Oprah said as she removed the black dress and revealed a red one underneath.

The sound of jingle bells came over the studio speakers, and fake snow rained from the ceiling.

"It's our favorite things! Ho, ho, ho!" Oprah shouted with an intensity that can only be described as *cheery sorcerer*. The stage behind her transformed into Santa's workshop, with PAs dressed as elves running around to make it look festive. The audience went absolutely wild. Comprised of 92 percent women and 8 percent gay men, the group looked like their heads would explode. There wasn't a ton of gay representation on television back then, but I remember feeling so seen when a man in an ascot raised his hands to the air as his legs gave out at just the thought of leaving that Illinois studio with a new Sony digital camera, panini maker, and Josh Groban CD. The entire hour was bliss, and it grew every year. Back in the late '90s, O was giving away pajamas, but by the 2000s, she had iPads and cars. One year, she did TWO(!!!) episodes of Favorite Things. Eventually, Oprah decided to retire her daily talk show, and we all cried as she said goodbye to daytime, and Kristin Chenoweth sang "For Good" at the United Center during her last week on air.

I lost sleep at night worrying about losing my Favorite Things episodes. They marched on, albeit in different form in her magazine and via Amazon.com, but it wasn't quite the same. I still follow, of course, needing to know what type of brownie pans Oprah says I should buy, but I long for the days of a studio audience losing their shit at a flat-screen TV reveal. Is it too much to ask for the Oprah Winfrey Network to gather some essential workers and give them refrigerators and Black Eyed Peas albums on camera? Maybe by the time you're reading this, there will have already been Oprah Favorite Things reform, and networks/streaming services will have realized that the best special they can give us during the late months is not a variety hour hosted by Miley Cyrus and Bill Murray but a reboot of these Oprah classic episodes.*

In the meantime, I thought I'd comprise a list of my favorite things for you all. These all make fabulous evergreen holiday gifts for you or someone you know.

1. ***How Do I Un-Remember This? Unfortunately True Stories.*** A book by me.
2. **Expensive bedding.** If you are an adult, you need to invest in luxury bedding. There are so many different levels, so you don't have to completely break the bank, but you should be spending slightly more than what naturally seems appropriate for your sheets, pillows, and duvet. You're in the bed every night, so it will all be worth it. Plus, if you're single, a cozy bed will attract a cozy partner. It's also imperative that a duvet cover should be filled with *two* duvet inserts. This is what makes it look pillowy.

---

* I would once again like to encourage ABC to reboot the Nick Lachey and Jessica Simpson family Christmas holiday variety hour that they did back in 2004, even though they are divorced and happily have new families.

3. **Seasonal body wash/candles.** I love a peppermint shower scrub or a sweet cinnamon pumpkin pancake three-wick, and so do most people.
4. **Food.** Specifically, I like frozen deep-dish pizzas from Chicago. If you're from the Windy City, chances are you have your favorites...I prefer Giordano's, but I know other people like their Lou Malnati's. Both places, as well as many others, sell frozen versions that heat nicely and make for a delicious treat throughout the year.

Detour

While we're here, here's a list of gifts no one wants:

- **Those baking mixes.** You know the mason jar filled with sugar, flour, and chocolate chips so the receiver can make their own cookies. Either buy the person cookies that are already made, or get them something else! No one should have to do extra labor to use your gift.
- **Something you must explain.** The person should open it and know if they like it or don't. It's always so awkward when your brother is opening something you got him and you have to say, "This is for your _____ when you _____."

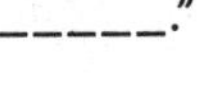

Finally, I have my perennial Christmas movie faves that I absolutely must watch once a year. It's not holiday time unless I watch *A Muppet Family Christmas,* a little-known Muppet special that aired in the late '80s. I know most Muppet fans prefer *The Muppet Christmas Carol,* which is lovely and wildly important, but the family Christmas special is always the most important for me. I get a little nutty about my Christmas movie watching, always scheduling time for both as well as another Muppet seasonal flick, *A Very Merry Muppet Christmas* (this one has a fight scene between Miss Piggy and Joan Cusack, if that helps sell you on its merits), plus traditional classics like *Elf, National Lampoon's Christmas Vacation, Home Alone 1–2, Home for the Holidays, The Family Man, Miracle on 34th Street, The Real Housewives of New York* Berkshires episodes, *A Diva's Christmas Carol, Just Friends, The Preacher's Wife,* select live performances from Christina Aguilera's *My Kind of Christmas* album era, *Meet Me in St. Louis,* Ashley Tisdale's performance of "Last Christmas" from a 2007 tree lighting, *The Santa Clause 1–3, I'll Be Home for Christmas,* and countless others.

My mom's favorite movie is called *The Gathering.* It's a 1976 made-for-TV Christmas film starring Ed Asner and Maureen Stapleton; most people have never even heard of it, but Linda worships it like it's the most acclaimed feature ever made. When we were kids, she would ask, "Who wants to watch *The Gathering* with me?" before sliding an old VHS into the VCR and curling up on the couch for a weepy family drama about Ed Asner dying and his grown kids visiting for one last Christmas.

My brothers and I would always turn down the invite, rolling our eyes at the idea of watching something from the 1970s that isn't *Rocky* or *The Godfather*. Eventually, she replaced the VHS with a bare-bones DVD, and when we would visit home as adults with significant others and kids, Mom would ask who wanted to stay and watch her *Gathering* DVD. We might've been older, but we were still just as uninterested in sitting through it. After thirty-something years of saying no, I finally gave in during the winter holidays in 2021.

Two years of a pandemic had just gone by, including social upheaval, elections, and all the other hellish things we'd gone through around that time, so I figured how bad could viewing one movie be? I suppose I was extra emo that year after not seeing my family for the entirety of the previous holiday season due to COVID. I was sappy, and relationships were put into perspective. So many loved ones were lost, the impact of which I don't think we've all ever properly dealt with, and I was just grateful to spend time with the ones I loved in the same room.

Mom and Dad popped some popcorn, I grabbed a blanket, and we started the movie. It was filmed in Chagrin Falls, Ohio, also near where I grew up, so Dad told me stories of his youth near the same waterfall we saw on-screen, and Mom shushed us at the right moments to ensure I didn't miss any important plot points.

We often get so caught up in our own worlds that we forget how to connect. We schedule catch-up phone calls to go through our troubles or list our accomplishments without ever emotionally connecting with the person on the other end of the line. Social media has separated us even more, so we tend to link up with people like us, which can be a great thing but also prohibits us from experiencing other points of view. The algorithm shows us only the people we agree with or occasionally the people who are so vastly different from us that it turns connection into anger. Politics pushes us left or right, religion becomes an excuse to dislike someone, and media capitalizes on segregating the "other." It might seem like everything wants to separate us, but pop culture remains the great unifier. Ask someone their favorite movie, and you might be surprised that a person who is of a different color or creed shares your fave. More than that, pop culture can help us relate to the people we love but have struggled chatting with.

After *The Gathering*, I asked my mom the other movies that meant something to her. She mentioned *The Way We Were* and *Love Story*, two movies from her youth I had heard about but had never seen. With everything at our fingertips, I was able to stream the movies on a lazy Sunday, then call home and talk to Mom about Hubble and Jenny. She seemed so excited telling me about her first time seeing them and her love for Barbra, and we related over the tears that resulted from the last scene of *Love Story*.

We attach memories to movies that move us emotionally, which is why, I think, holiday movies have even more impact than the traditional summer blockbusters. Everyone has their favorites; some prefer the slapstick of *Home Alone* to the romance of *Love Actually*. With the stress of the season, I encourage you all to take some time away from ice-skating and baking to ask your mom, dad, sibling, or friend what their favorite movie is. It doesn't have to be a Christmas flick, but if it is, sit down and watch it together. When the end credits roll, talk about why you like it, then ask them what it was like the first time they saw it or why they love it so deeply. It's so easy to find the things we all disagree on, but what are the things that make us feel like we're all living this human experience together?

After *The Gathering*, I invited my mom to watch one of my faves, *The Family Stone*, another weepy family drama centered on the idea of one last Christmas. The movies are surprisingly similar—grown kids with varying personalities visit home, where they're forced to say goodbye to their dying parent. It's all incredibly sad, and I wonder what it is about the holidays that encourages that trope. I think it's a reminder to the audience. We get so caught up in our worlds, and when December hits, we're expected to spend all this quality time with the families we've ignored for the previous eleven months. When we finally do see each other, it's filled with anxiety and stress. Yes, those movies are supposed to dramatically entertain us for a couple hours, but they're also meant to show us the alternative. *The Gathering* and *The Family Stone* are glimpses into our own lives; they're there to *It's a Wonderful Life* us into appreciating what we have when we have it. Some of you reading this might've already said goodbye and have a missing place setting for your holiday dinner, dreading the season without your people, but if there's someone, anyone, you have in your life whom you love now, take two hours and watch something with them on the couch. Revel in the moment together, whether you're watching some Hallmark hijinks or a maudlin festive drama, just appreciate being next to someone, and try to bond. Because in the end, connection is all we have.

Diet Culture

Food is always a huge part of the holidays. Throughout these pages, you'll find stories about hams and turkeys, cookies, and booze. It can be overwhelming for the average person, being faced with so many seasonal treats, and it's downright impossible for those of us who have food issues. This chapter is the hardest for me to write because it's the scariest. I feel especially vulnerable knowing it's not filled with pratfalls or hijinks to make you laugh but instead exposes a secret I've kept most of my life. If I'm being honest, this is something I wrote for my last book but was too weak to share through those pages. When it came time to turn in that manuscript, I deleted it, hiding the words on a separate hard drive, in hopes that one day I would be strong enough to share. Not sure I'm strong enough, but I am going to include it here, hoping that maybe one or two of you reading will feel a little less alone when you go to a Friendsgiving or office holiday party and stress over the menu and the hors d'oeuvres.

I was eleven when I was first confronted about having an eating disorder. Not even a teen, and people were speculating about whether I was anorexic. Before that, peanut butter was my friend, and we used to get together with M&M's on the couch quite a bit. When I was very young, the calories burned off me easily, but around age nine, they went to my hips and stomach and face and legs. Family would lovingly describe me as "chunky." Or if you were the father of my friend Tim after he had his day beer, I was "Chunk-a-Dunk-Fatty-Danny-the-Manny" (it was a tongue twister, but he managed). By ten, my parents pushed me to play football in the hopes that I would slim down to my previous size.

Most people think you need to be thick to play football, like being hefty would be a positive thing for the sport, but it turns out there is such a thing as being too overweight to play in the youth league. The first practice consisted of everyone hopping onto the scale in front of the rest of the team for weigh-ins. Out of roughly fifteen young men, three of us were deemed unfit...that is, unless we lost the appropriate amount of weight before the first game. It wasn't just a pound or two—I had to lose over ten pounds, which is a lot at that age. The humiliation of a youth organization labeling me overweight in front of all my peers was enough to push me right into diet mode for the first time in my life. There are plenty of things I don't know, but I've always been the type of person who is good at teaching myself stuff when I put my mind to it, so I excelled at dieting. Mom would take me to the grocery store, and I would read the labels on every last thing, always focusing on calories. That meant I wound up eating lots of rice cakes, vegetables, and powdered butter I put on baked potatoes and broccoli. I didn't care if what I was eating wasn't exactly food as long as it was low cal. I was obsessed and counted every single calorie that went in my body.

I felt completely in control, which I loved. Those of you who are type A know what I'm talking about: eating becomes a math equation. You know how many calories you want for the day, and you only eat foods with exactly measured portions. Eat less than the amount you pre-prescribe, and you lose weight even quicker! Hooray! Right? Health and wellness are so important, but I don't feel that a preteen should be as obsessed with calorie counting as I was at age ten. And while the other football players were concerned with tackles and throwing the perfect spiral, my every thought was consumed with ways to eat less. Pretty soon, I was dropping weight way too quickly. Over the course of just a few weeks, I lost more than fifteen pounds. And it kept going from there. Eventually, even the hand-me-down clothes from my older athletic brother finally fit me like they should instead of looking two sizes too small.

The more weight I lost, the better I felt. Girls in my class started paying more attention to me (which I thought I liked at the time, but...LOL, nope), and I didn't feel like the odd man out at practice. I was no longer the "fat kid" I felt they labeled me as, and my self-esteem flourished. I was even doing well on the football field—that is, until I almost passed out one day during a warm-up. Coach asked us to run some laps with our pads on. What I hadn't learned at that point was that food is also fuel, and you can't be very athletic with no nutrients in your body. I stopped and hunched over a fence with stars in my eyes and weak legs. An adult came over and tossed me some Gatorade—which I promptly drank after a quick glance at the nutrition label—and I pulled myself together.

"You okay?" the adult asked.

"I'm fine," I assured.

And that was the extent of anyone checking in on my health for quite a while.

When it came time for the next weigh-in, I'd lost more than the necessary amount to play the rest of the season. I should've stopped, but dieting was an obsession and hobby I wasn't quite ready to give up. I begged my mom to continue buying those chips with the olestra. They lit my ass on fire like a seasonal three-wick pumpkin caramel latte candle from Bath and Body Works, but they were fat-free! At dinner, I would pass on the delicious homemade food and opt for a rice cake. Queen Linda Pellegrino can cook, so saying no to her meals was a challenge in itself. Traditional dessert was a bust, but I'd save up my money for those cookies that came in the green box and promised zero calories, completely bamboozled by the entire diet industry. Even at a young age, I noticed people started treating me differently once I got skinny. A family friend who used to call me husky (and the man who called me Chunk-a-Dunk-Fatty-Danny-the-Manny) no longer did, I wasn't picked last in gym class, and puberty started to fill me out in the right ways.

Then something shifted as I noticed students start to whisper around me in school. The same kids who had called me fat were now critiquing me for being thin. I even overheard a couple of peers saying I had an *eating disorder*. I had never even heard the words before, and suddenly I was being diagnosed with it on the playground. My generation of young girls grew up with a deeper understanding of body image issues than I did (they were also presented with lots of fucked-up challenges because of the era and media; the women certainly had it harder when it came to weight/food stuff). One day toward the end of the school year, the phone rang. It was my principal asking to talk to my parents. Mom told me it was nothing, but I found out years later that they called to question my eating habits. The administration was concerned with my weight fluctuation.

When the football season ended in the early spring, we all gathered for an award ceremony in the gymnasium. All the fall sports players from each grade were there, along with family and friends who wanted to celebrate. Coaches got onstage, grabbed the microphone, and handed out awards to their best players in front of what felt like everyone in town. My head coach announced to the crowded room that I, Danny Pellegrino, won the MVP award for the football season. Me, the most valuable player! I was shocked and proud, but I knew I wasn't better than anyone else on the team. I joke about playing sports now, but I was legitimately a great baseball player, and my height gave me an advantage over the other kids when it came to basketball. Football, however, was *not* my game, but here I was receiving a prize for my work. What the fuck. Even as a young kid, I knew I wasn't being rewarded for the sport; I was being celebrated for getting thin. One minute, adults were worrying about my size, and the next, I was being congratulated for losing so much weight. And I was eleven years old. It forever altered the way I viewed my body.

My eating habits slowly got back to normal once I reached seventh grade. Probably a combination of feeling confident and my parents pushing a healthier lifestyle on me. Then, in college, I got it in my head that I needed to be more fit than I was. My peers were spending time in the weight room, and my hormones were leading me to check out all the other guys around me. I noticed the biceps I didn't have and the abs I so badly wanted. It all coincided with me coming to terms with my sexuality, and eating became something I could control when I couldn't control all that other stuff going on in my head. I started doing the calorie counting again. I took up running. There was no puking (yet), but I was definitely unhealthy. In between freshman and sophomore year, I took my dieting too far, and when I returned for fall semester, I started to hear the whispers again. People were wondering if I had an eating disorder. Clothes that once fit tight suddenly looked baggy on me, but because I couldn't see an eight-pack of abs, I continued to eat very little and run obsessively. That doesn't mean I didn't have an eight-pack of abs, just that my eyes weren't seeing it.

Once again, I got dizzy, and this time, I woke up in the campus hospital with my roommate looking after me. Lack of nutrients caused me to black out and faint.

This time around, I was a little bit older, so I knew when my diet was getting out of control. I saw the problem, and although it was hard to stop, I was able to curb my issues before they caused any permanent damage to my body. What I didn't realize then that I know now is that my obsessive personality is not an issue when it comes to loving TV shows or movies, but it is when it comes to my eating.

Off and on for years, I would take my diets too far. Every time a new Whole30 or Atkins came around, I would hop on the bandwagon. Unfortunately, no matter what I did, I was *never* happy with my body. What I see in the mirror is not what everyone else sees. During my fittest, the years in my twenties when I was doing CrossFit six days a week, I had the body I'd always dreamed of, but I couldn't see it. I can never see it while I'm in it.

During the really extreme times in my adulthood, I threw up my food. Calories in, calories out. It seemed logical. I learned sick tricks, like what foods to eat that easily come back up. If I had to attend a big dinner, I would pray they would serve pasta because I knew that was easy to vomit. It was never a regular thing, but even one time is too many, and it was more than one time.

A few years ago, I got a job ghostwriting a diet book. I'm sure a lot of you are thinking that sounds like a nightmare to someone with food issues, but it turned out to be a great experience because it forced me to learn more about nutrition. I had to know exactly what a carbohydrate is so I could write about it, and I had to learn how proteins and sugars work in the body. Diet culture only taught me about calories, but nutrition taught me about the bigger picture.

That's not to say I was all good after that. Before the aforementioned diet book came out, I was terrified. Most people would worry about the writing, hoping audiences would be satisfied with the work they did, but instead, I concerned myself with how my body looked. I didn't want to be the chubby guy who (ghost)wrote a diet book. I wasn't chubby, mind you, but that's what my mind saw and told me over and over. Body dysmorphia is similar to depression in that it can convince you of anything—you see a different person than the one in the mirror. I obsessed again in the months leading up to the book release, working out twice a day and eating small portions. I could've followed the lessons in the book and done it the healthy way, but I fell back on the same routine I was used to.

My weight has fluctuated in the years since, always within about twenty to thirty pounds. Just when I think I have a handle on it, something happens to throw me off. In 2020, some unrelated health issues caused my weight to go up and down what felt like every other week. The subsequent global pandemic didn't help my waistline either, but aside from those few previously mentioned periods of my life when I rapidly lost weight, I don't think anyone would ever look at me and think I had a problem with my size. I've always been active, and the heaviest I've ever been in my adult life is still not considered obese. Not only that, but I also genuinely like the way I look otherwise. I think I have a nice face, I'm more than satisfied with my height, and although I don't have the best fashion sense, I look handsome in a suit. It's the body dysmorphia I can't get over, the pounds my eyes see when it's just me and a mirror.

I wish more than anything that I could end this chapter by telling you I'm healed, but I'm not. I don't know if I'll ever be. And more than anything else in this book, I'm horrified for people to read this chapter. I worry I'm not talking about it in the right way or that you're going to think I'm forever unwell. This has always been my little secret, and now you're all in on it. I keep imagining others treating me differently at dinner parties, watching what I eat or wondering if a trip to the bathroom is a relapse. And the holidays are the hardest time, when food greets us at every corner. We indulge and overstuff our faces with turkey and pie. In my head, I bargain with myself, trying to reason that I don't have to reveal *everything* to you in these pages. Shouldn't some things remain personal? The angel on my shoulder is telling me I need to write this so some of you out there find some solace in my admissions, but the absolute truth is that I need to send this out into the void to come clean, to release the memory of the young kids on the playground whispering about my well-being. I want to emancipate the echo that swirls inside my head telling me my body is too fat or too ugly or too big. I pray these pages will help me love the skin I'm in, even just a little bit more.

Christmas Cheer

"Best way to spread Christmas cheer
is by singing loud for all to hear."

–*ELF*

Some years, I can belt at the top of my lungs and still be a Grinch. That was me the year of our next story. I made it through December 23 by going through the motions, but I couldn't go home for the holidays, so I spent Christmas week in California, where palm trees replace pine and the city clears out. I felt myself falling into a holiday hole of despair I couldn't escape. Determined to make the most of it, I called up my new friend Angela—who always seemed super optimistic—to spend Christmas Eve doing the most festive activities to bring me out of my holiday funk. She was alone this holiday season, and it always makes me feel good to spend time with a fellow lonely friend. Plus, my boyfriend had been working a lot, so he wanted to just vegetate by himself.

Angela is a coworker of my friend Sam. Sam invited Angela to her birthday party a few months earlier in August, and after a few drinks, I must've given her my phone number (or rather, the booze I sucked down decided to give her my number).

Our duet of "All I Want for Christmas" last night was epic! It's Angela by the way, she texted after that fateful first night together.

Sam's birthday party had taken place in a rented-out karaoke room, and although I don't remember singing *with* anyone (too many vodka sodas), belting out a Christmas song in the summer sounded like something I would do. Once a week or so, I would get a text from Angela, and all these texts were holiday themed. It was our connection. Sam warned me about Angela almost immediately, telling me to tread lightly with her. Apparently, everyone in the office hated Angela, but I figured office politics were none of my business. I'm sure plenty of coworkers have hated me in the past, so why not give her the benefit of the doubt? Sure, I heard she'd gotten caught faking a broken arm for three months to get sympathy from her peers and access to the disability parking spot, but c'est la vie! Besides, Christmas is a time of kindness and love and forgiveness, and Angela was always nice via text, so why not take the relationship to the next level? I invited her to my apartment for December 24, and I was optimistic I would be able to go from Scrooge to Santa in no time with the help of Angela and some activities that promoted holiday cheer. Yay, Christmas!

We started early. Angela arrived at my house around 9:00 a.m. with hot chocolate, the kind that radiates a deep, sweet aroma. Unfortunately, Angela wanted to save us some cals, so she'd bypassed the marshmallows, and when I took the first big swig, there were none to slow the flow, and I ended up burning the roof of my mouth.

"Sorry, I forgot to tell you I told them no marshmallows."

My tongue was numb, and everything I ate after was tasteless. Still, I marched on, ready to enjoy the day. Feliz Navidad!

Next on our to-do list was baking. I bought one of those cookie presses the year before on clearance but never used it. It's one of those devices that looks like a plastic gun filled with dough as its ammo. You're supposed to aim it at your baking sheet, then pull the trigger to release the dough. It comes with a variety of barrel shapes, so you can allegedly make cookies shaped like holiday items, but unfortunately, I didn't realize you had to use a special recipe with this product. My dough was too thick and heavy to use in the press, so the machine got clogged, and we never got any cookies in the oven.

While I was casually swearing at the press, Angela was trying to play Christmas music, but the Alexa robots in my place misheard her say, "Alexa, play 'Do You Hear What I Hear,'" and instead kept responding, "Yes, I do hear you. What would you like me to do?" like a sad, updated "Who's on First?" The holiday is about more than cookies and music, so Angela and I decided to just leave the mess and head out for ice-skating—an activity that would surely lift our spirits and put me in a jolly mood! Ho, ho, ho!

Well, first we had to get gas. But at seven dollars a gallon, the credit card machine was down, so I had to go inside to pay. (It turns out all the machines were down, except the ATM, so I had to take out money with a four-dollar fee just to fill up my goddamned gas tank.) Cheap-ass Angela told me she'd forgotten her wallet and her Venmo wasn't working, but I know she just didn't want to chip in because *suddenly* her purse appeared when we got to the ice rink and she wanted an Italian ice, but it was nowhere to be seen at the Shell station. I also opened the Venmo app on my phone and saw that the night before, Angela had sent ten dollars to our other friend Dave for "Getting F*cked Up" with an elephant emoji. I didn't say anything to her because, well, Christmas is the time of joy and giving, and I was being all about the love. (Speaking of giving, I did decide not to give her the gift I'd wrapped for her that morning. If she was making me pay for gas and ice-skating, I was keeping the pumpkin pecan-waffle candle.)

Ice-skating cost forty dollars each, which is fifteen dollars more than normal. Apparently, they raise the price on the holiday, which is such bullshit. Whatever. I was being cheery and paid the fee anyway. I don't own my own skates, so I also had to pay extra for those, and they didn't even have my size. The young woman working there handed me a size eleven even though I needed a size thirteen. "These are close," she said. I curled up my toes and sausaged them into the skates; otherwise, this trip and the gas would've been for naught, and I was determined to have myself a merry little Christmas.

It took me a little while to walk toward the rink because

the skates were so tight, and while I was bent over adjusting, Angela spilled some of her Italian ice on my head. Keeping on trend for the day, the bathrooms were closed, so my neck was sticky with lemonade residue the rest of the day. Still, I maintained my holiday cheer because it was Christmas and joy to the world or whatever.

Angela's icy treat was partially ruined, so she supplemented it with a hot dog. I thought it was risky to eat so much food from a concession stand, but she insisted. After only ten minutes on the ice, she started to get a stomachache from the concession stand beef and asked to leave.

On the way back home, Angela told me she had a gift for me in her car. I worried this meant I'd have to give her the candle—an item I got emotionally attached to keeping when we were back at the gas station—so when we got to my apartment, I went under the tree and grabbed an item I wrapped as a bonus gift, the kind of shitty gift you got and regifted to the mail person or a neighbor who stops by with cookies unexpectedly. It was a hot chocolate mix in a mason jar, which I figured would be good for Angela since it came with marshmallows, and she'd failed to put marshmallows in the hot chocolate that morning.

Angela handed me a perfectly wrapped box, and my mood began to turn. I even felt my smile curling upward. Until I opened it and saw it was a Blu-ray copy of *Die Hard*.

"It's a Christmas movie!" Angela said. Ugh, it's not to me, but also, pa rum pum pump um and stuff.

The only non-Christmas Christmas movie I recognize is

Last Holiday. There's nary a mention of anything Santa-related in that Queen Latifah movie, but the poster has the word *holiday* and Queen in a red dress, so it counts.

"Thank you. This was so nice of you," I lied.

Although I wanted to boot Angela from my house and watch *The Family Stone* for the fifth time that year, it was Christmas Eve, and I figured I should be nice like Santa or Jesus or whoever. I threw the hot cocoa mix at her and poured myself a shot.

"We should watch a holiday movie!" I said, trying to lift my spirits. A cozy flick to get us feeling like Scrooge after the ghost stuff.

"Yes, we can watch *Die Hard*!"

I wanted to say out loud that *Die Hard* is not a Christmas movie, but she looked at me with doe eyes, and I remembered her telling me it was her first holiday without her dad. He wasn't dead; he'd just flown to the Bahamas with his new girlfriend. But still, I felt bad because I'm a nice human who wanted to be jolly.

"Whatever," I replied.

Since it wasn't pre-2010, I didn't have a DVD or Blu-ray player readily available and was forced to rummage through my closet, looking for any outdated equipment that could play this bullshit movie that doesn't star Rachel McAdams and Diane Keaton. While I was digging for the antiquated machinery, my boyfriend must have spotted the wrapped present with Angela's name on it, because by the time I came back into the room, she was lighting the pumpkin pecan-waffle candle—the one I originally bought for her as a gift but decided to keep for myself after she stiffed me on the gas. Not only was I unable to take the candle back, but now she had *two* gifts from me, and all I had was an old-ass Blu-ray. I was livid. I obviously couldn't yell at my boyfriend in front of her, but I texted him, *Why the f did you give her that, fucking fuck.*

Unfortunately, after I hit SEND, I realized I accidentally sent that text to Angela.

"Did you just text me?" she asked.

"Yeah, it's a quote from *Die Hard*!" I lied again, hoping to fill the remainder of the day with the Christmas cheer I was determined to have.

"I don't remember that line! Good thing we're watching," she replied.

Once the Blu-ray player was hooked up, I put *Die Hard* in the machine and said a silent prayer to Mother Mary that at some point in the film, someone says, "Why the eff did you give her that, fucking fuck?"

Angela opened her hot cocoa jar and decided to pick out the marshmallows one by one while we watched Bruce Willis and company.

"I don't normally eat marshmallows, but they're kinda good plain," she said.

I'm not sure why exactly, but the way she ate the marshmallows made my blood boil. Since this was my year to have a demeanor as bright as Rudolph's nose, I forced a smile.

Twenty minutes into the movie, Angela fell asleep from a sugar crash, and her snoring filled the room with a sound I can only compare to elephant calls. At least I wouldn't have to explain the text dialogue thing. Meanwhile, my boyfriend was in the other room watching TikToks on his phone. I left Angela and went to check on him.

"What have you been up to?" I asked kindly.

"I've done absolutely nothing all day. It's been wonderful," he said.

"Do you want to do something Christmassy with me? Angela fell asleep."

"No, I'm enjoying just hanging out alone," he said.

"It's Christmas Eve! We're supposed to be in the holiday spirit!" I yelled. He wasn't interested. Why wasn't anyone as festive as I was? *Everyone else needs to get it the fuck together for the happy season,* I thought.

After storming out, slamming the door for dramatic effect, and calling my boyfriend a dick, I heard something that sounded like a crash come from the living room, and I raced over to see what happened. It was Angela farting. I'm not sure if it was the skating rink hot dog or the stale marshmallows, but whatever came out of her smelled like a dumpster and exploded louder than any of the gunshots coming from *Die Hard*. Somehow, Angela slept through it.

I decided I couldn't look at Angela for one more second, so I fast-forwarded the movie to the end credits and shook her awake.

"Movie's over. You fell asleep," I said.

"Already? I must've crashed," she replied. "Should we put on another Christmas movie? I think *Four Christmases* is streaming."

"I'm going to get ready for Christmas Eve mass. I like to connect with God to remind me what this is all for, how Jesus was born on this day," I lied.

"You're not religious," Angela reminded me.

"Right, but I'm just feeling kinda in church mode, so I thought I would go to mass today." I wanted to tell her to rot in hell, but I was channeling my inner wise man or Mary or whoever was in that nativity story because...Christmas.

Angela blew out her new candle and waited a beat for the wax to harden so she could take the gift that I didn't want to be her gift home. It was taking too long for my liking, so I put it in the freezer while she gathered her other things. She left a coat in my dining room, and when she was on her way to grab it, we found ourselves underneath some mistletoe I'd hung.

"We're under the mistletoe. You know what that means," Angela said playfully.

There was a voice inside me reminding me that mistletoe and friends are what the time of year is all about, and we're so blessed to celebrate the annual holiday...but I would've rather kiss a toilet seat than Angela in that moment, so when she pursed her lips and looked up at me, I swatted her away and blamed it on her hot dog–marshmallow breath.

I grabbed the candle from the freezer, tossed it to Angela, and escorted her out the door.

"What are you up to tomorrow for Christmas Day? Should we continue our festivities?" she asked.

"No, I'm flying to Ohio," I said.

"But I thought—"

"I bought a last-minute ticket while you were sleeping. Miss my family too much."

"Okay, well, have a wonderful Christmas, and let's do something for New Year's Eve," she said.

"No, bye!" I slammed the door and took a deep breath in.

My boyfriend took a break from his phone to join me just as I opened a bottle of wine I planned to take to the bed.

"Angela left already? Look, if you still want to bake cookies or do something Christmassy, I can..."

"No. I'll be in the bedroom."

"Pour me a glass. I'll join you."

"Grab a new bottle. This one is mine," I said, gripping my bed wine harder than Saint Nick grips his glasses of milk.

That was the last time I saw Angela. I never booked that flight, but I did spend my Christmas doing what I should've done all along: silently scrolling through social media in bed next to my significant other. Angela meant well, and I wish her all the best, but sometimes we need to be reminded that just because it's the holidays does not mean we need to be cheery or social. Sometimes other people are too annoying.

Season's greetings!

Blinks

One day you'll blink, and your kids will be grown.

That's the adage I've been hearing from my folks as they welcome more and more grandchildren to the family. They've said it for years now, but it's all finally starting to make sense. When I was a kid, time seemed to stand still as I stood by for jolly ole Saint Nicholas to leave the presents and take the cookie. I laboriously waited forever for December 25 to arrive. Now Aprils turn to Novembers in what feels like minutes, and those forevers seem like a lifetime ago.

I lived in a suspended adolescence longer than most. By my late twenties and early thirties, I was still stuck in that in-between phase, struggling in my career and barely able to make rent. I saw friends I'd grown up with purchase homes, have kids, and become their parents while I was still saving quarters for my local laundromat. We're never where we think we'll be.

Last year, I finally *did* grow up a bit, right on schedule for what life had planned for me. I moved into my first house, which almost didn't happen because, spoiler alert, moving is expensive! We made it work, and when Thanksgiving rolled around, my parents decided to join me and my boyfriend for the first Turkey Day in our new home, flying in from Ohio for a West Coast holiday, complete with light rain and unusually high temps.

"I thought we'd get a sunny holiday in California. What's with this rain?" Dad asked.

"It rains here sometimes. Last Christmas, it poured all day," I replied.

"Better than the snow," Mom added.

Over pumpkin pie, our worries floated away, and Mom started telling us all about her time caroling as a young girl in northeast Ohio. One year, she put a nightgown over her winter coat to look like a holiday angel, but the candle she was holding caught wind at a neighbor's house, and her nightgown went up in flames during the opening of "Silent Night." She used the snow to contain the flames and missed out on any serious burns, making it the perfect comedic tale to tell around the dinner table. This book is filled with my holiday stories, but we all have our own. No one escapes unscathed.

Mom and Dad reminisced about what it was like to walk past the tinsel that covered their childhood trees, static electricity forcing the decor to cling to their Christmas outfits. They remembered visiting Santa at Higbee's department store, Mr. Jingeling (a Cleveland mascot), mornings opening gifts with their siblings, and the special dollhouses and drum sets their parents had given them to make the holiday happy. I know

now that I'm older that with those good memories comes a lot of sadness. As visions of loved ones lost to time float through your mind, you're reminded of how much their spirits filled the rooms adorned with poinsettias and eggnog each year.

After the final bite of pie was consumed and the last of the dishes was cleaned, Mom and Dad packed their belongings and started to leave for the airport.

"Dinner was perfect. Thanks for having us, Danster," Mom said.

"Love you both! See you next year," I shouted back, knowing I wouldn't get to see them again until after the next ball dropped.

As they got into their rental car, I noticed Mom had left her bag inside. I grabbed it and ran out, waving them over before they drove off.

"Wait! You forgot your bag!" I yelled.

Dad parked the car on the side street, then rolled down the window, and I saw their eyes red from the tears that already streamed down their faces. They tried their best to hide the waterworks until after they got in the car, a tradition that started when I went away to college and continued like clockwork at all our goodbyes. They'd get in their car, or I'd get on a plane, and once I was out of view, they'd start crying. Occasionally, they slip up, and I catch the sadness on my shoulder from a hug goodbye, but no one tell them I told you that.

"One day, you'll blink and wonder where the years went," Dad reminded me through tears.

"We love you, my sweet son," Mom added.

I joined them in crying as I watched their taillights get farther and farther away. Another year over. Although it was the first Thanksgiving in my new home, I knew the lasts were right around the corner, and it finally hit me. A blink ago, we were living under the same roof, and in a blink, I'll be their age, telling my kids or grandkids or nieces and nephews the holiday stories from my youth as we bite into our pie. I'll tell them about the first time I hosted my parents for dinner, the lump will form in my throat as I talk about how fast time moves, and I'll bawl as I say my goodbyes, trying my best to wait until I'm out of view. I hope that at the back end of their blinks, the memories will be merry and bright, and when they sit with their children and grandchildren, friends and loved ones, they too have a story to tell.

Hopefully, their stories will be just as perfectly imperfect as the rest of ours. We're not always carving a glistening cooked bird around a Pottery Barn dining table or trimming a ten-foot-tall tree with popsicle stick ornaments and candy canes, and December 25 isn't always the Hallmark snowscape we've been sold since we were kids. We don't always have people to share our holidays with, and sometimes we're surrounded by people we don't like all that much. We've all lost loved ones and gained some others along the way, but there may be years in between when we're all we've got. Don't beat yourself up if you're preparing for a special day of crying under the covers instead of caroling with hot cocoa. Maybe you're dateless on New Year's

Eve or going through a breakup while your buddies are buying engagement rings. Some holidays will be joyful, others won't, but we just need the number of good years to outweigh the bad in the end.

As important as it is to hold on to the memories, it's equally crucial that we let go of the impossible standards we set for ourselves every time fall turns to winter. The ideal we've been promised doesn't exist, but *your* perfect kind of holiday does. I've worn snow boots to trick-or-treat; there are times morning show anchors sweat from high temps during the Macy's Thanksgiving Day Parade; and in December, all the romantic holiday movies look like the inside of a snow globe—fluffy white flakes swirling around the screen—but we often get the mushy stuff instead, the kind that usually forms as spring creeps in. Sometimes it rains on Christmas.

Acknowledgments

First and foremost, I'd like to thank the reason for the season, JC... Chasez. The *NSYNC lead was one of the songwriters behind the fabulous "Merry Christmas, Happy Holidays." We thank you for your service, my turtleneck prince™.

There was an old sitcom in the '80s called *Mama's Family*, which initially was a sketch on *The Carol Burnett Show*. Thelma (a.k.a. Mama) Harper was played by Vicki Lawrence, and on an especially memorable holiday episode, Mama befriended a goose named Leland she planned to cook for dinner. When push came to shove, Mama couldn't kill the bird and instead served her guests something else for the special occasion. Life doesn't always work out the way you plan. So we pivot. We serve mock goose like Thelma Harper did. All that's a roundabout way of saying I never could've imagined all my family holidays would be fodder for a book of stories like this one. Somewhere along the way, I took a new road that led me here. And if I never imagined it, I'm certain the loved ones in my life didn't anticipate it either, so I want to thank them all, everyone who is mentioned by name or description throughout these pages. I'm incredibly lucky to be surrounded by so many people I love *and* like. I may not ever be able to repay the family for letting me air our dirty laundry, but to help soften the blow, I decided to publish a seasonal drawing courtesy of my niece Sophia. Sophia forgot to put the *as* in *Christmas*, which I think is fine since I put the *ass* in Christmas throughout this book. Fingers crossed the cuteness will make everyone forget about anything they're mad about.

My forever holiday plus-one, Matt, thank you for the other drawings in this book and for putting up with me during the writing process. I love you.

Thank you to everyone at Sourcebooks! And to my incredible editor Kate Roddy, I'm forever grateful to you for believing in me and these stories.

Kristyn Keene Benton, my agent, and Brittany Perlmuter, my manager, thank you for everything!

Kenny G., I'm sorry I was so hard on you every time my mom played your holiday album back in the day. Moms in the '90s were right; it's a beautiful piece of work, so thank you!

Mariah Carey and the Muppets, thank you.

Finally, thank *you* for reading this book.

Happy Halloween

Happy Thanksgiving

Merry Christmas

Happy Hanukkah

Happy Kwanzaa

Buon Natale

Feliz Navidad

Joyeux Noël

Felizes Festas

Glad helg

...and a very happy New Year to you all!

xo, Danny

About the Author

© Brian Kaminski

Danny is the *New York Times* bestselling author of *How Do I Un-Remember This?: Unfortunately True Stories*. He's also a comedian, actor, and screenwriter who created and hosts the hit podcast *Everything Iconic with Danny Pellegrino*. Guests include Drew Barrymore, Kelly Ripa, Keke Palmer, Katie Couric, Rosie O'Donnell, Elizabeth Olsen, Andy Cohen, Cameron Diaz, Miss Piggy, and more!

Danny is from Solon, Ohio, and can be found on social media via @DannyPellegrino or in front of the TV with a glass of bed wine. His Christmas tree stays up at least until early January, sometimes much longer. 🎄